30
16
180
30
480

David

echoed "istad of "sa"

$400.⁰⁰ × 10 = $4000

FREE ME FROM ME

"CHAINS WERE MEANT TO BE BROKEN."

Have this ALWAYS POSTED!

MODULE 2

SHELIA MALCOLM   email them!

Boundary Setting
Bill of Rights   Old Patterns / New patterns

week 1   What is a boundary?
What are social boundaries
social creative boundaries?
relationship boundaries
common "

Scripture on boundaries?   Show diagram pattern changes Book.

Week 7: ~~What are~~ Setting personal boundaries.
Bill of Rights

What will you/will you not allow.

What is your swinging door
   "   "   " bolted door
        door w/a copy of your keys.

Different doors diff. boundary definitions per person or type of person.

Bill of Rights
Week 8: Narratives in the Bible characters who defined/ did not define boundaries + consequences.
LOVE/LIMITS
Respectful conflict
Stories share in group.

Week 9: Identity + Boundaries do they intertwine! Do they make a connection?

Assertiveness Training
MODULE 3

Week 10: Lets look at examples
of assertive behavior,
Lets define it together!

Jesus examples was He assertive? Heroes of the Faith, biblical
characters who exemplified
assertive behavior?
Lessons learned ....

Week 11: Assertiveness Dialogue (wk 12)
practicing / role-play →
↓ Light situations / semi uncomfortable

Effective Communication Building Part 1
Relating   Biblical stance

*I dedicate this book to my first grandchild, <u>Grayson</u> Bennett
Patterson; for being the gift that symbolized the breaking of the
chain that kept me bound for years.*

Week 13: Training part 2   → (wk 14)
Medium-stress dialogue,
↓ behavior / unconf. situations

Effective Commun. Building Part 2
Relating   Biblical stance.

Week 15: Identity, Boundaries,
Assert yourself   / ART THERAPY
Workshop. <u>Crescendo</u> Moment
~~Combo.~~

16
Week 17: Graduation celebration
Mindset Thrive: Completion of ~~PART 4~~
start date end date - Modules 1, 2, 3
X ___   16-week Educational
Workshop

TABLE OF CONTENTS

ACKNOWLEDGMENTS

To my mom, Florence May Bucknor-Ruddock, thank you for allowing Grandma Jane to raise me. For almost 13 years my grandma modeled the trueness of compassion and a heart for people like no other I have ever known.

To my beloved sons, Johnny and Mattheu, thank you for pushing me to Be! To walk my talk in reaching higher each day of my life. To not be afraid to live on purpose. To become the change I am waiting on.

To my friends on my 'front row'—Joyce, Stephanie, Londa, Vanessa, Jerome Stone, Errol, Mary, Grace, Millie, Daniel, Rachel, Jeannie, The Melliphant & Wolfe Family, The Cattnell Family, The Jenkins Family, The Lewis Family, and Dr. Sherley St Pre, thank you all for being the wind beneath my wings.

Thank you, Ed DeCosta, for asking me, "What is your gremlin?

Each person mentioned in the acknowledgments helped me hold the hammer that broke the chain.

FOUR PILLARS TO FREEDOM

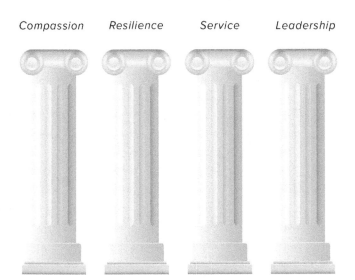

Compassion *Resilience* *Service* *Leadership*

INTRODUCTION

I WANTED TO WRITE A book as a memoir to my grandmother, Jane. I began writing in 1998, two years after my grandmother's death. I wanted the world to know about the champion who raised me. She was compassionate in her interactions with me and gracefully served others in the community. I wanted everyone to know how she effortlessly demonstrated resilience and leadership. I would not be who I am today without my navy blue-eyed, one-dimple grandmother. She fostered the depth of love and compassion that exudes daily from my heart.

From my conversations with her siblings and older relatives, I was reminded that I was between the age of one and two when I went to live with her. I'm not sure of the reason that brought me to live with my grandmother (GM). Looking back over my life, I am forever grateful that God's mighty hand was clearly involved. My journey began in Mi Jane's arms. Mi-Jane is the endearing name we called her. My GM chose to raise me because I was her first grandchild and even though I was not around my father or mother, I did not miss them emotionally. My GM made me feel secure and loved. She constantly told me wonderful things about my parents.

One of the first quotes she taught me was, "If you can look

up, you can get up." Grandma Jane handled adversities with style and finesse. She blazed through her tears often using them as fuel. I watched her consistently rise from the ashes of adversity like a Phoenix. Even though she taught me how to overcome, I found myself chained to secret kryptonite that kept me in oppression. For many years I would raise my head and see my possibilities, and like a turtle, I would quickly withdraw back into my shell. I believed that people would judge me because they would not understand the invisible pain I carried. My kryptonite told me that people would not be able to comprehend how a church girl raised in a good home could have made such poor choices. In the Jewish culture, turning thirteen includes a rite of passage where children transition from adolescence to adulthood. This is a huge milestone. For me, thirteen was a time of confusion, a time of wandering, a time of questioning and a time of being lost in my wilderness of emotions. As you scroll through these pages, you will learn about me and my journey, from where I was to where I am now: a place where I am resolute about who I am and my purpose in this world.

In 2012, I was in the gym on the treadmill running and watching one of those early morning shows. There was a story about a girl that had sex with many young men from a particular sports team at her college. The Bible tells us that "joy comes in the morning" but there was no joy for her that morning and many mornings to come. She was being made fun of and ridiculed for her mistakes. Things were being said that were not true. Her life would never be the same because of that incident. I felt the pain in her eyes as she wrestled with the reality of her situation. As I watched the story continue to unfold, I became angry. Almost instantly my anger turned to pain. Emotions took me over and tears began to flow down my cheeks like a tidal wave. For a split second, I had flashbacks to my abortion at age 13 and another at age 19. I wondered if people who knew me as cheerful, encouraging, and animated with a great big smile knew where my strength came from. Did they understand my past and how I got to the point of a genuine smile? Would they be forgiving if my past came out across the media as this girl's story did?

As I continued to weep for her, I realized I was weeping for myself. I cried because I wished people would really extend grace for the poor choice made in youthful years. Seeing the girl on the screen reminded me of my bondage. That day unearthed my sensitivity to the challenges of poor decisions made so many years ago and the false realities I chained myself to. I tormented myself with mental beat downs, replaying guilt and broken promises. The inner turmoil grew as I reminded myself of a promise to remain a virgin until marriage. Realizing that I fell short and did not keep my own promise to myself, terrorized me on the inside. It hit me with low blows in the pit of my belly when I made the same mistake twice, all from the place of shame and fear. It has taken me years to realize that no matter how simple your experiences may seem, these small experiences can be like a diamond in the rough when you need them most. From that day forward, I decided to come face to face with myself and forgive myself for the past mistakes of my youth. I wanted to be free from myself.

Even though I wanted to tell the world all these things, there were other things I did not want the world to know. Years ago when I began writing my story, I wanted it to be flawless. Once I entered the world of freedom, God would not let me write half-truths. Each time I tried to be superficial, God stopped me. There were things in my life I did not want anyone to know. Things I wanted to take to my grave as my grandmother did for me. But God would not have me write a book and tell you all half-truths. So, He stopped it! Over the years since 1998, I picked up the paper and pen more than a thousand times and got nowhere because I refused to uncover what I swept under the rug. It was not until my marriage of twenty-four years fell apart, and I moved to Florida that I decided to face my truth fully. I could no longer run forward without bumping into my past. God would not give me rest. This is how bad it was. I began to take inventory of my life and all of the painful experiences within it.

One step at a time, the journey to freedom continued with intentional actions to heal my wounded heart. I cried out to God daily, wrote in my journal and went to divorce care. The dam really broke for me when I enrolled in Life Coaching School. In Psalm 56:8, God promised to catch my tears in a bottle. So, I gave Him several bottles to fill on my journey to recovery. More than anything, I craved to be made whole; I no longer wanted to hide behind my shame. In the process of learning the art of coaching, I had many opportunities to be the client. During these sessions, you could either create fictitious scenarios or make use of your own story. I chose to keep it real and use my truth; this was a hallelujah moment for me. When I sat in the seat as the client, I opened the jar of teardrops; the pain flowed freely from my eyes. I was excited to no longer be trapped inside. Thank goodness for the big box of tissue nearby to absorb the salty streams that were aiming for my lap. It was during these sessions of answering the self-awareness questions that I gathered the confirmation of my purpose. I found strength in overcoming my issues, and I desired to help others overcome theirs, too. As I became free, I realized that every experience had worth. When we are honest with ourselves, we can appreciate the lessons learned through our pain. The more I healed, the better I became at telling my truth, unapologetically.

Eventually, I realized that my story was for God's glory even in moments where I didn't see value or worth in sharing it. I was always honest enough to say, "You don't know my story!" whenever people praised my outer appearance of strength and passion when praising God. My passion came as a result of my personal belief and dedication to love God wholeheartedly. I have been forgiven; therefore, I honor God much. I became a great teacher when I learned how to shift my perspective and praise my way through the journey. As I learned to fly with wings of freedom and purpose, I came to realize the power of my story. It has given me a voice of confidence for those whom God has assigned to me. When I speak, the passion within causes them to move. It empowers them to chase their freedom! I stand firm on four pillars developed during my personal process of forgiveness and freedom. The pillars remind me of my paternal grandmother who modeled a woman I wished to become someday. Each of the pillars began with seeds planted through the teachable moments with my Grandma Jane. I eventually exuded the behaviors I saw in her and became the chip that fell from her block. This apple did not fall too far from her tree; I am the fruit of her labor.

I no longer cower in the corner, bound by shame. My freedom empowers me to claim my place in the world. So I implore you to take inventory along the journey I will share with you. I freely give the lessons of my journey and the joys of my grandmother with you. It is now 35 years after my first abortion and I embrace the fact that the path I took those many years ago was to help someone break free. If that someone is you, let's find the hammer and break your chains.

COMPASSION

"The Foolish man builds his
house on sand ... The wise man
builds his house on the Rock ..."

—Author Unknown

UNSHAKABLE FOUNDATION

ONE OF THE MOST COMPASSIONATE moments I can remember with my Grandma Jane, was when I was about five years old. We were at the river and she was washing clothes for the family. It was a Sunday, I remember the day because she had a routine. That was the day she washed. I was not feeling well. To make me comfortable, she spread a brown weaved Crocus bag on the bank of the river. She wanted me to sit there until she completed her washing. I had my doll and snacks to keep me entertained. After waiting a while for my grandmother to complete her washing, I grew weary and tired. Since I was not feeling well, I wanted something else other than my doll and snack. Like any child, I called out with desire, "Mi-Jane, I'm thirsty, may I have some water please?" *Mi-Jane* was an affectionate name family and friends called her. She stopped scrubbing the clothes on the scrub board to figure out how she was going to get me water.

She rose from the bending position over the white enamel tub and placed her hand on her hips. That was her default position when she had to think. She looked left, then right, trying to figure out how she was going to get the water to me. Immediately in front of her on the opposite side of the river bank near the edge were some plants with big leaves. These were dasheen bushes. An adult could fold the leaf and dip it in water, and the leaf would serve as a temporary cup. Unfortunately, I was too small to hold it without getting wet. Removing her hands from her hips, she stepped into the waterhole in the river, collected the water in her mouth and brought it to me and poured it into my mouth. I swallowed and was refreshed. She went back to her washing, and I waited some more until she was done. I did not think about it then, and it took me years to understand it fully. That was one of the many acts of kindness my grandmother showed me. When I am homesick, I daydream about my childhood on the island of Jamaica. I started to have flashbacks of some events in my life while growing up, and I felt my grandmother in my heart. If someone were to ask me how to measure love, I would say, "I don't know. But I know for sure is that my grandmother loved me." She may not have said "I love you," but her actions throughout my life conveyed the ultimate gift of love which she bestowed upon me.

You will hear threads of our relationship throughout this book. I want you to be present with me as I share the stories of our interactions. I don't remember many things about my childhood, but from what I can remember, I thank God every day for my grandmother. She was the Rock I needed, the smile I needed and the gentle touch I needed to chart my path for today's result.

As a child, I remember I loved her dimple, and I often played with her face looking for her dimple and wanting one to come on my face. As unique as her eyes were, so was her gift to love. She loved her children, me, her nephews, her nieces and people in the community just about the same way. She loved us all with compassion. Her smile and her eyes spoke to us. You could never ask her for something, and she would say no if she knew you really needed it. Her name was given to her mother in a dream. As you know back in those days, there was no such thing as a sonogram. However, her grandmother had passed away before she was born. One night as her mother slept, she had a dream, and in the dream, my GM's mother dreamed that her mother said: "You are going to have a girl and you must call her Jane." She was the only girl amongst four brothers. She was a precious stone among her brothers of rubies. Although she only had a ninth grade education, you could not tell because she was smart. She had a great memory, and she was extremely hard-working. She had a great business sense. She used all of these gifts to bless her siblings, her children, her brother's children, extended family's children and me.

As a child when I cuddled with my GM, my hand was often in her bosom playing with her warm breast as she rocked me slowly and sang beautiful soothing songs to me. Who would not love that position? It was a place of comfort and peace. When I think of her, I smile and cry all in one moment. I smile because I was blessed to have her in my life and I cry because I miss her so much. When I think of those precious moments we spent together, my mind goes back to the time as a young child when I was thirsty; my GM carried water in her mouth and gave it to me as a mother bird would feed her young. As I share these stories with you, I am right back there in the very spot where the action took place, experiencing the feelings all over again. Each time I experience the emotions, I am reminded of my foundation and the pillars of my strength. As I sit and contemplate my childhood on the islands, I find that there were many expressions of my grandmother's compassionate heart which she extended to me.

Like all children, I liked sweets and candies. I can remember sneaking sweets at night by placing them under my pillow in my bed. I would happily brush my teeth and say my prayers to rush to the sweet treat tucked away in my bed. Whether it was a Milo, Horlicks or paradise plum (one of my favorite candies), I could not wait to enjoy it when my Grandma Jane, wasn't watching. After a long time of eating sweets without getting up to brush my teeth again, the evidence ultimately showed up in the form of a toothache. On the islands, when people felt sick, they self-diagnosed, and they would try home remedies first, before going to a doctor. When my toothache started, my grandmother did not take me to a dentist right away. She naturally tried home remedies first. As I developed a full-blown cavity or two, after consistently eating sweets without brushing, I started to feel the pain more severely, especially at nights. Grandma Jane would try using several options to soothe my pain. She would crush Bufferin or Panadol (painkiller tablets) and stuff them into the cavity. If that did not work, she would try rum on a cotton ball and saturate the tooth and gum line surrounding the tooth. Once this method was applied, she would rock me in her arms for hours while sitting in a straight back chair. As I wrestled with the pain, she soothed me by singing to me until I drifted off to sleep.

Growing up in Jamaica, my grandmother did not have a comfy couch that's found in many homes in America. So, she would sit in the hard wooden chair with a soft cushion on the seat and rock me and sing to me, night after night, which told me she loved me. Even though I was the cause of my own pain, she made it her mission to comfort me, even at the cost of her sleep. This comforting process happened over and over again until she felt my pain was now too much. She determined this by the number of interruptions I had each night and the lack of rest we both received. After many sleepless nights that month, she decided it was time to have the dentist remove the tooth. All these molecules of kindness were building blocks to my unshakable foundation. When I would fall and bruise my arms and legs, as the tears flowed down my cheeks, she would say, "Hush, it's going to get better before you get married!" even though I did not know when I was going to get married. But I trusted her and soon, I would stop crying because she washed my wounds and added some medicine that burned but soon cooled off so I could run off and play again.

After my GM's children grew up and left the home, she raised a nephew, a cousin and me. As our faces differed, so were her unique ways of making all of us feel special. We each had our own towels, our specific eating utensils and anything we could own individually, GM made sure we had them. To my GM, owning your own things was important. She did not want anyone complaining that someone did this or someone took that. We each knew what belonged to us and we had to take care of it to make sure it lasted us a long time. She wanted us to respect one another and what we owned. This was a lesson in being an owner and not a borrower. When we could not find something, she did not want any of us to blame anyone else because it was an individual's responsibility to know where their stuff was. One of my GM's rules which I still use and say today to my children: "If you put it the same place every time you can find it even in the dark." When it was time for my bath, I had my personal soap, towel, toothpaste. These toiletries were not allowed to be shared with anyone else. I cherished this lesson because it taught me to be organized and to be responsible. When we could not find the specific things we owned, she did not help us to look for it; she would say, "I told you where to put up your things, now you can't find them, you'll learn next time. Do without and keep moving."

Since I was exposed to a healthy balance of compassion in my youth, I tried to find it when the support beams of my marriage started to crumble after 24 years. There were many issues that disrupted the foundational level of my marriage. Like a newly-built home, many times after a year or two you may see cracks appear in some of the walls. The builder may say it's due to the house settling into its foundation. My marriage was past the two-year mark. This crumbling was not to be ignored because the foundation was shifting. In the midst of my emotional mess, I decided to peel the onion skin of my life, layer by layer. The more I peeled, the more I found.

At first, I started to point fingers and play the blame game. But, as I continued to take inventory, boxes of tissues pulled up right beside me to keep company with my paper and pen. I kept asking questions. I kept praying, and I did the work. I looked up! I could not get up, but I looked up! I was no longer willing to stay where I was. I could hear the voice of my grandmother as my tears flowed like an overflowing dam and washed the mahogany floors in my bedroom closet. My tears brought to surface the truth of what I was running away from for so many years. I needed to *offer myself compassion and forgive me.* I forgave other people in my life like my mother for not raising me with my other siblings. I forgave my father for being so far away and not knowing him beyond a once-per-month-collect call. I was able to let those emotions go toward my parents, but I struggled to forgive Shelia.

The breakthrough moment came for me on August 25th, 2012 on the mahogany floor in my bedroom closet. My heart had already accepted my decision to leave my marriage, but my feet were delayed in making the move. That Saturday morning was not very different from any other Saturday morning. However, I want to believe that my unconscious being took over and allowed time for my conscious body to come into agreement. When I woke up that morning, I did not say, "Today is the day I will leave my husband." I did not even think about it. I can't really tell you exactly what happened in the moments after hugging my husband as he walked out the door to church. I told him I would meet him at church. I never got there. As I ascended the steep staircase to my huge master bedroom on the second floor to get dressed for church, I felt a sudden shift in my body as I climbed each stair. When I finally got to my bedroom, I started to walk toward the window near my closet. Tears welled up in my eyes really fast. I could hear myself repeating over and over, *"I can't do this anymore. I can't do this anymore."* With the rhythm of every word, I started to pull my clothing off the hangers in my closet. I remember reaching with outstretched arms and pulling random clothes from the hangers. I did not realize the strength with which I yanked a dress off the hanger, yet, with that momentum, I slipped onto the floor and there I stayed in a ball until my heart stopped racing. Feeling the shift in my body, I knew it was time. It was the day to leave. I felt the strength that my GM so often modeled for me. I grabbed hold of the hope that I saw her use so often as a support beam to stand to my feet. I took some clothes, my personal documents, like my passport, citizenship paper, birth certificate, four of eight $2 bills from the fireproof box where we kept all our important documents. Then I removed several favored pieces of black artwork from the walls in my bedroom and my basement and started to load my little burgundy 1999 Hyundai Elantra.

As I made a few trips back and forth to my car which was now parked in the driveway for easier access, I interrupted my flow to call my sons on a three-way conference call at their University to tell them that I was leaving their dad. My older son pleaded with me not to leave. He suggested I wait until his dad got home and then leave. As good as his suggestion sounded, I told him that I could not do that. As a matter of fact, I told him, "There is no good way to leave. Whether I left now or later, so I think it's better while he is not here." After my call with my sons, I called my sister to come and help me move, "I am leaving my husband today," I told her. She understood the urgency in my voice, she asked no questions. She sent her husband to help me because she was not able to come. I called a friend in the nearby town and asked her to keep some of my belongings in her garage until I got myself sorted out. She agreed. When my help came, I wrote a note and left. As I was driving down Interstate 287, I knew that the possibility of me going back to my home was almost zero percent. The reality of that thought conjured a pipeline of tears once again. It was during that moment that I recollected it was the 16th anniversary of my GM's death. It was very telling that the end of a marriage was like a death. Mourning was expected in both events as part of the healing process. How ironic it was for me to take such a drastic step to exit my marriage as I reflected upon the loss of my GM so many years ago. But still, at times, it feels like yesterday to me. I don't know if it was a coincidence or not to leave my home on the anniversary of my GM's death. But in hindsight, it was a twist of fate.

I held on to hope as my anchor to move forward, and I would not let it go until I *Free Me from Me.* That was the life-changing day I took responsibility for my past mistakes and committed to myself that I would not settle on any level anymore. I recognized I wanted more out of life. I was going to get more by giving more of me and become more authentic to the world, starting with me first. It took many test runs and me falling back into the arms of *fear.* I was determined to break every chain in my life because chains were made to be broken. I kept remembering the words of my grandmother in my mind. She was and still is the greatest cheerleader in my life, as a matter of fact; she is my She-ro. I don't know if I could have been as strong as others saw me to be if I had not chosen to take a page from my GM's book. My GM provided me the example I needed to make some tough decisions in my life. I had a blueprint to follow. That blueprint was, "Even though it's hard, do it anyway." Power through the pain with my tears and all that comes with resilience. I literally heard her compassionate, soothing voice in my inner consciousness say, "Shelia, you can do this!" If you can look up, you CAN get up! Les Brown made this quote famous, but I thought it was my grandmother who created it.

The compassion I experienced from my Grandma Jane was not evident with my father. I came to the USA in July 1981 to live with my father, stepmom and two younger siblings when I was 13 years old. This is a very interesting age for any child to start a relationship with their parent. My father was a "do as I say without discussion" kind of a guy. His personality prevented me from having a great father-daughter bond that I so yearned for. Even though my grandmother loved me dearly, she believed in the saying, "If you spare the rod, you'll spoil the child." My grandma was small in stature, but when the time came for her to discipline you, you better watch out. Let's just say I was afraid, very afraid. I felt her love for me without question even in moments of discipline. My father, on the other hand, was a totally different story.

I wanted the kind of dad where I could feel safe to ask questions about life. I wanted to be able to talk to my dad about my dreams, what he thought about me as his daughter and hopefully touch on the subject about boys. I did not think that that was too much to ask. Every girl wants to be daddy's girl. My father did not have any sons, and I was the oldest of his three girls, so I longed for the time when we could just hang as he fixed his car on the weekend. I wanted to pass him the tools or even go for walks on the boardwalk near our home.

As I matured, I came to the realization that it was important to have a relationship with one's dad. I wanted to hear my father say, "You are beautiful," or "I like your hair," or "I like the dress you are wearing." But that did not happen, so I tried different ways to connect with my dad and improve our relationship. Unfortunately, I can't tell you we had a great working relationship; it was rocky at best. There were many days when it seemed like I took one step forward and he took two steps back. This emotional dance went nowhere. However, I continued to pursue it and showed respect, even though it was not always reciprocated as I wished. As I became an adult and started a family of my own, I made a vow in my heart to become a better parent when I had children even if it *killed* me. Building relationships was important to me then *and* now. After experiencing the kind of love and affection my grandmother so generously gave me for the first thirteen years of my life, I didn't think it was too much to ask the same of my dad. If my dad walked into the room at this moment and sat in front of you, you'd immediately notice his powerful stature. You might even become instantly grateful that you didn't have to live with him. He wasn't mean-spirited; he was just too serious. To me, my dad was so handsome when he smiled, but he rarely allowed his smile to appear. He always had neatly groomed sideburns that handsomely caressed his jawline. If he relaxed and seemed to be enjoying life, he could be on the cover of GQ Magazine. Sadly, the memories I recall of my teenage years with dad are of his critical spirit more than his praise. He was quick to tell me what I did wrong like putting two creases in his jeans and shirts when I ironed them. Or when I cooked his scrambled eggs too hard for breakfast. I could not even get a "good job" for passing a test or a class with eighty percent. So many days I wondered why I had to have such a firm father. I did not always appreciate it; neither did I realize how valuable the demonstrations of his strength would be in my life. It was only when I became an adult that I chose to look at my father's actions through different lenses. I had to shift my mind-set and tune into the lessons I learned from my father's disconnection.

The major takeaway for me was using what my grandmother showed me in the early onset of my life and what I experienced with my dad to develop compassion. In retrospect, I can now appreciate the differences between my grandmother and my father. Both have played a key role in my unshakable foundation. Some characteristics I have cherished while others have been discarded.

Grandma Jane was compassionate in reminding me of my worth relentlessly as a child. She cautioned me to reject any opinion that did not highlight my value and potential. She knew that thoughts were powerful and consistently encouraged me to always think that I could make it, even in moments of doubt or fear. She ended her life lessons by telling me that I was a survivor. She placed a protective layer over my life. Each of her affirmations still lives inside of me today. Every foundation faces a test, no matter how firm.

As the proud mother of two wonderful sons, I see the world a bit differently now. From day one, I decided to make it my duty to have an exceptional relationship with each of them. When it came to building our relationship, I knew that one style would not fit all so, I was very purposeful in treating each of my sons as the unique individuals they were with compassion. I became conscious of the disconnect my father and I had, and I remembered the void it left in my life. I didn't want my children to experience that same feeling of emptiness and disconnection from their parents. I was very intentional about the words I used to correct them when they made mistakes. I was and still am their biggest cheerleader to offer them compassion with words of encouragement as they strive to become who they were created to be. As a mother, in my earlier years, my focus shifted from myself to the foundation for my children. I needed my children to be strong men with balance and valor. I learned to show affection in simple things like a morning greeting or evening text as they matured. At the end of my day, I greeted them and asked how their day went and truly listened. These were things I missed in my foundation with my father. I shared my past mistakes and successes with my sons to help them understand that their mom was human. I've learned their personality types so I can offer them the best possible resolutions. I also encouraged my husband at the time to be better to our children than our fathers were to us. I wanted him to be purposeful about everything in our lives so we could create the best environment for our sons.

We may not be able to change people or our past, but we can change ourselves and our actions. When we change ourselves, we can succeed in becoming better people and parents. I learned a few tough lessons in my role as a mother, sister, friend and wife. Sometimes I doubted my own strength, and I would have to revert back to my grandmother's words. I could not allow how I felt to stop me from moving forward. As I go through life even now, I experience many tests and trials but I've come to know that perseverance is the partner I need on the road I must travel. I stand firm on my unshakable foundation with all its cracks and chips. A life without test does not exist, so I fix my eyes on my faith and plant my feet on the firm foundation. Just like me, you may someday come across people that will test you. For some, it may be a boss, for others, it may be a friend, a spouse or children. In those moments of doubt, when you are forced to question your worth or your value, remember you are worth more than anyone can pay. The challenge will be, to believe it on the inside with all of your heart. This must be buried deep down inside of you that no matter what circumstances come your way, you can resurrect the knowledge to say, "I am worth it—I am a survivor." When you walk down the street or in a room, there must be a sign across your face that says: "I know who I am." Just knowing your worth helps you from being beaten and battered by the negative words people will say that will cut like a knife and cause you to become a wounded soul. Having strong self-esteem is your bulletproof vest that will protect you from life's gunshots.

As humans, we are not always aware that our tongue is one of our greatest weapons. When words are spoken, they can either elevate you or cut you down like a sharp axe. Whatever the words, we must be compassionate in our correction and intentional in our action.

On Saturdays or Sabbaths, my grandmother always went to church. She would sing, giving praise to the one true God who had continued to bless her. As a child, I had to sit next to GM in church and pay close attention to whoever was presenting from the front. If I chatted with the kids nearby, my GM would give me a nice little pinch all in love to bring my attention back to the front. Most things being said up front was "way over my head" as it was not spoken in language for children to understand. My GM would do all these responsibilities with such joy. I never heard her complain. She would even sing while performing some of these very chores. Sabbath was a special day. After church, we got to eat the lunch GM prepared from Friday evening and kept warm by the fireside in the hot ashes. This was an art GM mastered with the power of Jesus. The foundation of faith was required for my growth.

Foundation is indeed a key component to living a life of freedom and faith. If your foundation is firm, the rains and the storms will come, and when the sun decides to show its face, you'll still be standing. Be kind to yourself. Even if you were not privileged to have a Grandma Jane as I was. She crafted the pillars and paved the way for my unshakable foundation early in life. I had to reflect and learn how to be kind to myself first by nurturing the seeds of compassion in my mind, and I challenge you to do the same.

MINDSET

"If you're not riding the wave of change . . . you'll find yourself beneath it."

—Author Unknown

IN ORDER FOR ME TO embrace what I believe to be my destiny, I had to become courageous enough to take inventory of my life. I knew that my first step was to change my perspective. I started with my mindset! I did a deep dive and asked myself some difficult questions. I recognized that if I were to live my destiny, I had to see things as they were! Not better than they were, not worse than they were, just as they were! Self-examination allowed me to see what was holding me back as I wondered what I would do if things were different. I acknowledged that my mindset was crucial to getting me out of my own way. The more I examined myself, the more I realized the bondage in my mind. I chained myself to my past, and this held me back. Mindset is the building block of beliefs and thoughts that shape

ask Shelica

your life. How you think determines what you feel and how you feel affects what you do. Mindset impacts how we make sense of the world around us and how we see ourselves in it.

I started to write my list in response to my *what-if question*. What would I do if money was not an issue? This question popped up first. *Why*? I was living in a place of scarcity. I had the physical evidence of scarcity all around me. My financial overview at a glance reflected an upside down mortgage. Letters from collection agencies piled high on my kitchen counter. Even more evident, I carried the baggage of a scarcity mindset. Having financial challenges overwhelmed me to the point of daily frustrations. The day I answered this question, I discovered that ideas started to flow. It was now limitless as to things I wanted to do. Things I *could* do. I began to dream again. I did not wait until I went to sleep. I started to dream out loud. I became bold about things I wanted to accomplish for many years but did nothing about them. Now there was a shift. All it took was the first step toward honesty.

When I was a teenager, not much shorter than I am now, an adult family member told me I needed to change how I walked. They felt that I looked like a lady of the night (yes, a prostitute) because of how my hips swayed as I walked in my three inch heels. Can you imagine that? How does an adult say something so hurtful and damaging to an impressionable young person? That statement stuck with me throughout my teenage years. I carried that hurt inside. Many others poked at me with other words that wounded me but there was one difference between me and the rest of the world; I had an unshakable foundation. My grandmother engraved a sense of self-worth in my mind, but I was unable to unchain my emotions from shame. I could not shift my mindset from the heavy chain of shame to freedom.

Many topics, especially sexuality were not talked about in church. Outside of school and church, I went nowhere else as a young girl growing up. How could I get the answers to the questions I had about sexuality? The church is supposed to be a place you go to get answers but what do you do when only certain questions get answered? When sexuality questions go unacknowledged, sinful discovery is the alternative.

As a teenager, I thought of myself as the "ugly duckling" with acne zits across my face. I just wanted someone of the opposite sex to love me. There was more to me than the marks on my face. This was my teenage desire. One late night in 1990, an associate told me that she was contemplating suicide because her then live-in boyfriend left her with their infant child and married someone else in their home country. I felt her anguish as she sobbed and shared her broken heart. A sense of empathy came over me, and I led with my heart again instead of my head. I thought sharing my story would keep her off the ledge. I think it did, but it ricocheted to my shame. The associate now thought she earned the right to peddle my story after she regained composure from her broken heart. This experience sent me like a turtle into my shell. The shell that had said that I would not talk about my shame of abortion anymore. Talking about it opened wounds that had not healed. Thus, if I wanted my wound to be healed, I must not talk about it again. This was what I told myself. I kept that promise for many, many years. It was now a secret tied even tighter than it was before. I promised myself no more. It hurt too much to be vulnerable in an attempt to be authentic. Shame can affect your personal life and have a domino effect on your profession. Shame in your personal life can keep you from climbing the corporate ladder or advancing in your career. Shame can be a stumbling block, and your future can be stifled by the mistakes of your past. As status in career elevates, the possibility of being out-front is very definite. Once you are out-front, your personal life is no longer your own. You are now held by a different standard and personally under the microscope. You are scrutinized by the thoughts and opinions of the public. If there are things in your past not known to the world, you are now a target of this information being found out. It can then become a 'field day' by the public critics. If you are not built with the strength of iron, these private details coming out can destroy you. Not because you lied or covered up, but because you failed to be authentic and vulnerable with the mistakes of your past.

Sometimes I look over my life and revisit the poor choices I made. Many times I can't find a good reason why I did it, nor can I find anyone to blame. The only thing that keeps coming up is, I was afraid. Fear can cause you to make some stupid choices. Not once but multiple times. I have asked myself time and time again over the years. How did I get pregnant? And I have found no good answer. I told myself at a young age that I would wait until I was married to have sex. But I was naïve. Sex was not talked about in my home. My grandmother taught us about God, good manners, respect, survival, good hygiene, hard work, education for a good job and love. Sex was not in the curriculum. Neither were there any discussions about the development of my body as a young girl. I had no idea what to expect. I did not understand the physical changes in my body.

Living on the islands in the 70s, there were lots of older women in the church and the community that could have provided guidance to me and other teenagers, but no one talked about sex. It was a forbidden subject. It was off limits. I felt like it was a sin for anyone to even say the word sex in the church and even worse from the pulpit. Growing up with no male figure in my life to teach me or to talk to me about the masculine gender was a rude awakening. As much as I wanted to have the conversations and ask the older women questions, I could not. Listening to and watching my older female friends talk about their relationship experiences; I secretly wanted to understand what they talked about. I grew up in a very loving home, rich with values but 'sex talks' were off-limits.

The little I learned about my body and sexuality was from my attempts to eavesdrop on conversations among the older girls. I remember the youth ministry's program at church mentioning a book called *On Becoming a Woman* by Harold Shryock. The book talked about sex, puberty and womanhood and was marketed as a suggested reading for the eighteen and the older. There were no books available to me as a newbie in the teenage world. Grandma Jane worked hard to keep me out of the company of young boys and older men, but we never had any formal discussion or teachings about "the birds and the bees" or how to relate to the opposite sex. This subject was somehow a taboo in many sub-cultures during that era. The belief at that time was that if the subject of sex was talked about, it might send the wrong message. The elders believed the discussion would promote the exploration of the behavior.

I grew up with two male cousins who were both older than I. They were very protective of me. None of their friends were allowed to treat me any differently than a little sister. In their minds, they were protecting me from being taken advantage of. I believe that the lack of a masculine voice in my life as I grew up caused me to submit to the attention I received from males. I did not have a male to tell me what to expect from other males, or how to understand and to respond to their conversations.

As a young teenager, I surrounded myself with girls older than I. I think after hearing so much about what they did, I wanted to know and experience it, too. I wanted to see what it was like, but I did not know how intrusive it was and how my life would change because I was so inexperienced. My mindset was tainted with the belief that if I asked them about the 'birds and the bees,' they would think I was 'wanting to be grown.' I would then be asked, why do I want to know? The lack of knowledge was supposed to be a safeguard for children to not become sexually active. Keeping things a secret, with no discussion or sex education classes in the schools or the church made me even more curious. Whenever the topic of sex was mentioned, it was said to be 'for adults only' not for children; but no one took the time to discuss with children about their changing bodies from adolescence to adulthood. I can speak for myself, up to the age of 13; I knew nothing about sex education.

My menstrual cycle started when I was thirteen. Grandma Jane kept close tabs on the dates and the duration each month without my knowledge. She was very observant, but I thought I could get by without her noticing. She referred to menstrual cycles as "friend," and when the month came, she asked me if my "friend" had come to visit me. Grandma Jane knew something was off as I hesitated and began making excuses. An unexplainable fear surrounded me as the moments of interrogation grew longer. Knowing what I had done, I cried and trembled uncontrollably as she became the ultimate detective in the living room. If my responses were not loud enough, she yelled for me to speak up. As she became enraged, each yell was followed by "you think you are grown." Holding the leather belt in her hand, she transformed from my sweet Grandma Jane to a hurting mother. Her eyes filled with sadness and her spirit bathed in anger as she said, "I am going to help you realize you are not grown, you are still a child." She wanted all the details without delay. If there was any hesitation, the belt met me across my back. She wanted to know when we became intimate, where it took place, and how many times. The questions were coming so fast that I could not quickly formulate replies.

My mind was frozen as my emotions and body experienced the pain of the moment. I cowered in defeat while trying to explain the frequency and beg for forgiveness for the "accident." She launched a complete review of her weekly schedule trying to figure out how I ended up in this uncharacteristic predicament. Grandma Jane paused her schedule review to retrieve his name because she knew everyone's parents in the neighborhood. Her anger boiled over into an explosion as she found out that it was someone my family knew very well. He was the son of one of the elders in our church and a brother of one of my friends. If it had happened today, he could have gone to jail because he was 20 years old and I was 13. Once the interrogation ended, Grandma Jane delivered a spanking, which I would never forget. She quickly implemented a contingency plan to protect me from further involvement with this young man. My grandmother did not explain anything further. She put more stringent rules in place like; I was not allowed to stay home by myself or with my male cousins without her being present. If I could not go with her, she would drop me off at a relative's home to stay while she was gone and pick me up on the way home. She applied rules to protect me from the boys at church, in the community or any other place boys would be. I could no longer go anywhere and tarry later than she expected. She would give me a specific time to return when I had to run errands.

If there were meetings at church for the teens, I had to go with a group or an adult who was going. She would pop up unannounced at the location I said I was going to be. She would walk down the road to meet me when she thought it was time for me to be on the way home. I was under the microscope, and she was not letting me off the hook any time soon. I lost the little freedom I had.

Grandma Jane's mindset shifted because she did not want me to mess up my bright future. She did not want me to become like many young girls who had babies early in their lives and were not able to finish school or get a job to provide for themselves. This was a secret we kept hidden to protect the possibilities of my future. Besides my grandmother, only two other friends and the young man's parents knew about "the accident". I would make up a story to guard my secret if I became emotional. I kept my silence because no one was supposed to know except the one that was imprisoned. Many times, I battled with the voices that were crying inside for help. "I'm broken! I'm burdened! Can you hear me yelling?" No one could because it was all in my head. But it was audible to my heart. When the guilt was overwhelming, it sounded like cymbals clinging together as alarms to remind me of what I had done. I wished I could undo it, but I couldn't, and I didn't know how to forgive myself and let it go.

When it comes to the issue of shame, somehow it is not considered as terminal. For those who have experienced shame like me, we can tell you that shame sometimes come dressed up in stomach issues, ulcers, acid reflux, nervousness and so forth. The body develops these sicknesses because we hold everything inside. We are too frightened to address our chains with others because we are afraid of rejection. I chained myself to a mindset that encouraged bondage and brokenness. I am sharing my story to bring about healing to my fellow believers in the pews who want to live an intentional life. To be authentic comes with a risk. If you don't have a high tolerance for pain, being authentic will be an uncomfortable place for you. Therefore, I told myself this statement, "If the church is a hospital, let us use it for what it is designed to do. Let us stop pretending with a fake smile while the lid of our anguish is about to flip over with a bang." Once I faced my past, I was able to move forward, allowing myself to embrace each day. With God, there is always an opportunity to bounce back.

God is very smart, compassionate, kind and forgiving. I have learned to intentionally take time to reflect on my life's journey with gratitude. God gives us very distinct experiences in order to awaken and reveal who He is to us. We are all created in His image to reflect His light to every human being we encounter. Whether we touch them physically, virtually, emotionally or spiritually, I can tell you that as I embraced the experiences of my abortion, I was taught *compassion*. The ability to cross the figurative street and walk on the side of no judgment has given me an empathic heart. God provides clarity through experiences to create teachable moments. These teachable moments are lifelong lessons that leave imprints on the heart. These imprints are not easily erased. Carrying my secret baggage of abortion held my tongue when I wanted to make a critical statement about another woman.

"Evaluated experience is the best teacher." This statement is coined by world-renowned leadership teacher and mentor, John C. Maxwell. Before I make a derogatory remark about someone, I check myself. If I am honest with myself and want to improve my character within, I won't want to make judgmental comments about others, knowing that my experiences have humbled me. I realized that I had to change my mindset, from a fixed mindset to a growth-oriented mindset. In a fixed mindset, I told myself that things could not be changed. When I took the courageous step to embrace a growth-oriented mindset, it liberated me to now believe that my abilities could be developed through dedication and hard work.

I challenge you to consider the lessons your life's journey has taught you. If you have not learned them yet, grab a pen and a piece of paper, sit quietly and look within. Take a moment to write out each answer. Read them through, take in the responses you get in your quiet moment. Make peace with what you learn and move forward with the lessons as the light to guide you on the path you can create for betterment. Stand firm on the unshakable foundation with compassion and a positive mindset and nothing will be impossible; this I know for sure.

RESILIENCE

"Until you make the unconscious conscious, it will direct your life and you will call it fate."

—C.G. Jung." Ed DeCosta

BREAKING THE CHAINS

I OFTEN WISHED I KNEW how to find the weakest link to the chains that held me hostage for so long. All the while as I grew up, I kept searching for a way out. I did not find it until it became clear to me that only *I* could break the chains. It was only then that I could embrace the cause of my fight for my freedom. During my search, I began to understand that education was the hammer I could use to free myself. I eventually realized that going to school to get a high school diploma or a college degree was not enough for my life. I needed to learn and truly understand me. I was clueless about my true worth and value as a woman. Being book smart is wonderful; however, to make it in life, one needs more than book savvy. We *must* complement the knowledge with understanding. Holding my realization close, I began a quest to understand and educate myself about myself. I knew that my freedom so desperately hid behind the truth of my chains. I was willing to go to extreme measures to be free because my bondage no longer suited me. George Washington Carver said, "Education is the key to unlock the golden door to freedom." Oh, how I needed that key to the door of my cell! Had I known then what I know now, my stay would have been shorter.

As a Christian, I believe that nothing happens before its time if it's ordered by God. I can only embrace that now, looking back and digging up buried bones from the graveyard of shame and regret. Little did I know that that which I had gotten rid of in the past would now speak wisdom to my soul. We use the cliché, "the church is a hospital"; if it is, why aren't the sick being attended to? When I say sick, I use the term loosely. If my sickness is not obvious where others can look at me and see me literally bleeding, then I may not be considered as someone that needs an I.V. or immediate care. I know the church is not an Emergency Room, but if we refer to it as a hospital, is the ER closed to those who are hurting? Is it closed to those who have symptoms of a serious onset of an emotional?

Who said there is no jail time for an abortion? I served two consecutive terms in my self-made penitentiary. All because I lacked the education necessary to be my guidepost to help me navigate the path of being a woman. The journey to freedom through education began in a familiar place, High School, my alma mater. John Dewey said something very profound about education. He said, "Education is not preparation for life, education is life itself." I wholeheartedly concur with John on this quote. When I started learning how my body worked and developed, I gained a new perspective on how fearfully and wonderfully I was made. I packed my pain away, buried deep inside in the locked corners of my soul. I was raised in an environment that promoted secrecy; we did not tell our business. My grandmother always cautioned me to keep my personal business private. I adopted this mentality and held on to the false truth that no one needed to know the dreadful details. I often heard the elders say, "Just keep on living," and for years I became a skillful pretender, wrestling with my inner turmoil. Even in my pretence, I could not avoid the unintentional reminders of the choices I made. A simple news feature of women telling their stories about choice sent my emotions into a frenzy.

Radio commercials trying to reach young girls who were unsure of what to do with the growing seed within them brought tears to my eyes. Billboards displaying pictures of what a baby looked like from conception to birth made my stomach churn with unease. The advertisements tugged quietly at my heart each time I listened or saw them. I can remember feeling the paralyzing grip of guilt that stopped me in my tracks. Though my outer appearance was collected, controlled and polished, the deep emotions tugged at my spirit, causing my tears to create a salty zig-zag path from my cheeks to my mouth, and landing on my laps. This quiet storm was repeated several times before I made the choice to release the feelings of guilt tightly tucked away in my soul. I wanted to break free from the chains of despair in the prison of defeat. Grandma Jane showed me resilience, and life forced me to apply it. Breaking the chains meant that I had to find my hammer and dig my way out. This required me to come face to face with my past and take back my power.

Coming to America and living with my father created major post-abortion challenges. When I came to the USA, I came into a readymade family with a father who was practically a stranger. While I was growing up in Jamaica, I would call my dad periodically from the public phone in the town. The calls were mostly to keep him updated on my progress in school. Surprisingly, one day while walking with my friends to the bus stop, a car approached us with a man driving and a woman in the passenger seat. He pulled up next to me and said, "Hello." I politely responded. "Good Afternoon, sir!" He asked me if I knew who he was and I said, "No, sir." He quickly replied. "I am your father." I said bye to my friends and entered the car and headed home to my Grandma Jane. I remember this as if it were yesterday, although it was July of 1981.

My dad carried mysterious energy that has always puzzled me. He had a good job at JFK International Airport as one of the diesel mechanics with the company, allied for more than 15 years. He earned a decent salary and was a good provider, but I wanted more from him. He was good about taking my sisters, stepmom and me out to dinner at the best restaurants. Whenever we went out to eat, his daughters were not allowed to order anything from the menu that we would normally eat at home. The normal kid foods like a hamburger and French fries were forbidden at the fine dining tables. Dad would point out the filet mignon or grilled fish with a baked potato for us to select. He wanted us to experience new foods at the restaurants we visited. Dad was also a sharp dresser, and he made sure we experienced some of the sharpness in our dressings, too. We lived in Brooklyn, NY, and the winters were very cold, so my dad made sure each of his girls had a sheepskin coat to keep her warm. The part that puzzled me about my dad was that he was good about certain things related to our care yet in other areas, he was almost non-existent. When I needed my dad to communicate and help me understand him and his personality more, there was silence. I wanted to know that I had his undivided attention when it came to discussing things about my personal life. I wanted an emotional connection with my dad. The kind of connection that I heard about from many of my friends when they boasted about their relationship with their parents. I could not contribute to the conversation truthfully. Many times I would stay quiet and just listen, or sometimes I embellished stories about my dad; most times I wished they were true in my heart.

He was very focused on academic excellence but lacked the capacity to show affection. He held me to a high standard and test results less than 100% were not acceptable. His intentions might have been good, but the environment was unhealthy. No matter how great I thought I performed academically or otherwise, he always said I needed to do better. I cannot remember any instances where he offered positive affirmations or praise for a job well done. I always felt like my best was not good enough and I could never make him proud. The unrealistic expectations affected my psyche, causing me to think that I could not satisfy my dad unless I was perfect. My dad wanted his daughters to have the best and be the best as far as education was concerned. However, there was a missing link in my dad conveying that to me. He was very disconnected and unable to contribute to our success, especially when it came to building relationships. My experiences with my father created chains of fear and insecurity within me. The emotions that originated from the constant insecurities I felt aborted my joy and my peace of mind. It caused fear to constantly whisper in my inner ear things I wanted to forget.

When I graduated from high school, I became intoxicated with optimism as I nurtured unrealistic anticipation of connecting with my dad. As I prepared for college, I tried many times to forge a conversation with my father about men and relationships. He declined and refused to entertain any discussion of that nature. He rather defaulted to his academic expectation, cautioning me to "stay focused on my books." When I pressed the matter with an obvious desire for guidance, he set a clear standard in saying that no man could come into his home as long as I stayed under his roof. That statement pushed me further away from my father and deeper into my shell. The lack of guidance created a chain of resentment while forcing me to "figure it out" alone. The disengagement from my father plagued me all the way into adulthood. This was one of the reasons I struggled with knowing what to look for in a male partner.

College was a new world for me. I met so many young men and I quickly developed a romantic relationship. Keeping the relationship from my father was a true test for me. I longed for attention on the emotional level, my yearning was obvious, and I easily entered the sexual aspects of my relationship because I craved connection. I became pregnant shortly after my relationship began and before completing my college education. Immediately the chains of fear began to shake in my mind; my father would not accept this. My boyfriend at the time offered no support and soon broke off the relationship with no further contact. My mind was unable to process the overflow of emotions. The chains of fear squeezed me tightly while causing me to believe that this was an impossible situation. Facing it alone caused my insecurities to take root and grow stronger. Fear eventually won the battle and created a new chain of shame within me. I was yet again crippled and bound to the vow of silence and secrecy. This was when my second prison term with abortion began. Chains of despair developed shortly after that college crisis. I grew tired of feeling like my back was against the wall while my emotions ran wild. I no longer wanted to own the chains that bound me in the private prison. My memories of Grandma Jane's resilience gave me the strength to unpack my cell and face myself.

At age 19, my boyfriend left me alone to deal with my decision after he found out I was pregnant. In his selfishness, he only thought of himself and not me. I chose him over me. It was always about him and what he wanted. Yes, I compromised and put him first ahead of me. It seems that was my demise because this was a repeated mistake, until one day, I woke up and said, 'Enough!" grandma Jane went to her grave with my secret. She protected me all the way to the end. That's what love is.

If my grandmother walked into any room right now, you would instantly see her deep dimple caressing her right cheek as she greeted you with her beautiful smile. Without hesitation, I am confident you would want to take her home with you immediately. My grandmother, just like most grandparents, was mostly fun but you would know when the fun time was over and when it was time to be serious. Things seemed to always transition smoothly in my grandma's house. The only time you would be confused is when she was about to give you a quick lash for something you forgot to do or when you disobeyed. She would always smile even as she delivered your spankings. She never spared the rod because she did not want to spoil the child. One of the biggest and most important things I learned from my grandmother was resilience. No matter how devastating a situation was, she always bounced back, with strength and power.

I remember seeing Grandma Jane sitting in silence one day with tears streaming down her face. No sound, just silence with an occasional sniffle in between her teardrops. I watched as she lifted her head from its lowered position and wiped her eyes with the hem of her skirt before continuing on with her chores. Her silence left me wondering what could have been the cause of her tears. My cousins and I later connected the dots when she called us all together to question us. Grandma Jane asked if we had friends in the house without her permission. My older cousin said no before grandmother tearfully revealed why she asked. The money she was saving underneath the belly of the sewing machine was missing. She had intended to take the lump sum of money to the bank in town the following week. Almost in unison, we all replied by saying we did not take it. Grandma Jane knew we did not take it. However, she struggled with wonder about who could have done it if we did not allow friends into the home. The mystery continued for many months, and a portion of her money was always missing when she retrieved it to go to the bank. This constant loss was very aggravating to my grandma.

Eventually, the mystery was solved when a family friend visited our home unannounced and saw a family member who lived in a nearby district exiting our unoccupied home. Through her wisdom, she was able to put certain behaviors together and figured out who the culprit was that had been taking her monies from the house all these times. Even though the mystery was solved, she was heartbroken because it was her own relative and not a stranger. The amazing thing about this incident was that my grandma did not disconnect herself from this relative. She continued to relate with him even after finding out he was stealing from her. I didn't really know how she handled it because again as a child, I could not ask her for details about the matter. Reminiscing on the resilience which Grandma Jane modeled as she faced adversities, came to my aid many times as I grew into an adult and had to make tough decisions. Grandma had to let go of her anger with her relative who stole from her, and she was able to still have a relationship with him. She had to forgive him.

My father passed away in 2002. That was a tough time for me. I had lots of mixed emotions. Less than a year before my dad passed away, I started to see a gentler, kinder side of him as he visited me in my home. He wanted to spend time with his two grandsons. I welcomed the change in his attitude and stayed away from any questions that could disrupt the new person I was experiencing. Shortly into seeing this new version of my father, he became ill from diabetic complications. While he was sick and in the hospital, I had many questions to ask him. I wanted answers and possible closure. For years I carried the questions in my heart when I remembered speaking to dad days before my wedding. We talked about what he was going to wear to my wedding, but all along, he had other plans to cause disruption on my wedding day. I had looked forward to the day my dad would walk me down the aisle even though I knew we did not have the perfect relationship that I dreamed of and wanted since childhood. I wanted to know why he never came to my wedding. I wanted to know why he called other family members and told them not to come to my wedding.

Eventually, I called my stepmom and told her I was thinking of talking to my dad about the lingering questions. I wanted desperately to understand, but due to the sensitivity of my dad's ailing body, I decided to wait until he recovered. However, his health turned for the worst, and once he passed, I had to pick up my questions and make a decision to let them go, permanently. I turned to my stepmom and asked her why she thought my dad tried to sabotage my wedding. She had no answer, and she suggested that I release the unanswered questions that hindered my progress. My stepmom was divorced from my dad for many years before his illness, and she confirmed that my dad loved us in his own way. The steps toward forgiveness were extremely difficult, but I had to do it so I could move forward positively in my life. My dad was no longer here, and no one could answer my questions for me.

Again, I had to rely on the tools my Grandma Jane used to get through the tough times in her life. I cried, prayed, and then cried a little more. My Grandma Jane passed away many years before my dad died, so she was not here to hold me or attempt to rock me in her arms in the straight back chair anymore. But she did leave me her legacy of strength from the unshakable foundation she created for me so many years ago. In due course, I found someone who listened and provided encouragement to keep pushing through for my freedom.

In 2012, for the first time in my adult life, I shared my past with my best friend, Joyce. She was compassionate and prayerfully understanding as I spoke of the abortions. As I found my hammer and began to break free from the past, I painfully sobbed. She held the phone and counted it a privilege that I chose her to share it with. I remember hearing her offer thanks to God as I wailed and whimpered on the other end. For as long as I can remember, she has always practiced thankfulness. No matter the situation, she finds the strength to thank God for every breakthrough, big or small. More so the small ones!

Joyce is my sister-friend and the only other person in my life outside of my grandmother that prayed me through with love. During my sharing session with Joyce about my painful past, I was also drifting and waning from my 21 years of marriage. It was not just a good emotional time in my life. There were so many things to deal with on an emotional level that I broke down. I did not break into pieces or have a nervous breakdown, but I did break my silence. I no longer wanted to be a prisoner to my past and peeled back the onion skin to find my freedom. My own husband at the time did not know about my abortions. I held them all inside because they were my chains.

As I struggled to free myself after sharing my story, it felt like all hell was breaking loose in my life. Things were all out of control, and I could not seem to keep my grasp on my finances or my challenging emotions. My mind began to spin out of control, and the downward spiral happened faster than I could comprehend. One morning on my way to work along a desolate winding country road, I felt pain radiate from my chest. This was a turning point for me as I refused to let the weight and stresses of my life situation kill me. I wanted to live for myself because I loved life, and I wanted to live for my sons.

In very sentimental moments, I have flashbacks of my sons, especially the birth of my firstborn, Johnny. On that particular day, I remembered his beautiful eyelashes and allowed my mind to rest in the beauty of God's creation. I saw God's matchless grace with Johnny in my arms, and I saw God's grace allowing me to hold that which I had gotten rid of so many years before. I truly realized then that God is a God of a second, third and many more chances. All I had to do is just ask Him. Imagine, if you were able to experience something you did not ask for, oh my! You'd jump out of your seat with praise and thanksgiving!

God did not stop at one for me; He blessed me 17 months later with another son that was almost washed away. I was taking a lot of medicines that could have aborted Mattheu because I did not know I was pregnant. When I finally went to the doctor to confirm why I was not feeling like myself, he told me that I was several weeks pregnant. This news did not fit into my plans, and

I struggled with trying to figure out how I would take care of two small children in diapers all at the same time. Many questions flooded my mind as I wondered when I would rest and how could I love them both equally without favoring one over the other. I had serious dilemmas going on in my head, and I felt bombarded. I thank God for my husband, who at the time brought me back to reality by asking me, "Aren't you married?" I could not find the words to answer him as he asked me why I cried at the news. Little did he know of the turmoil in my head about having to take care of two babies! I felt overwhelmed because I needed to rest and return to work. Fear swallowed me as I replayed thoughts of being unable to handle the responsibility of the growing child inside. I resorted deeper into my self-controlled thinking and chained myself to sadness, not once thinking to run to God as I was having my meltdown. Thank God He knew best and eventually calmed my spirit while reminding me that He was there to help me. Now I go to God on a regular basis to ask for guidance and direction as I deal with the issues of life. I relied on myself a lot back then and limited my freedom to my knowledge. This was one of the instances where I learned resilience. God knew I could be a mother to two beautiful sons before I believed it. But I still needed to unpack the wounds and break free from the chains of depression, abortion and divorce.

FREEDOM

I OPENED THE DOOR TO freedom at a training event for the John C. Maxwell Certification in Orlando, Florida on August 11, 2015. I went to a workshop which I thought was going to help me with marketing skills. About half an hour into the training, I realized the workbook had nothing about how to market my skills. What this training *was* about caught me by surprise. I had no idea that this would be the day of my break-through. The trainer, Ed DeCosta, asked the group to identify their personal gremlins. I heard the question and kept reviewing it in the booklet, but I could not seem to respond. My uncon-scious mind put up a fight as I tried to flip the page and bypass the question. I felt my heart begin to race as the internal noise grew stronger with each passing moment. Eventually, I found the courage and calmed my nerves enough to write down what was holding me back. There was this one gremlin that stood in the way of where I wanted to be. This question opened the floodgates to a number of responses. The internal battle was raging on the inside as I did my best to keep my cool. I was so afraid to expose my gremlin because I believed that the folks in the group would think less of me if I shared.

After a few minutes of silence as we worked on the task, Ed

asked who wanted to share. My hand went up involuntarily. In my heart, I had no plans to share, but God had a different plan. Ed called me to the front of the room. Tears instantly began streaming down my face as I cried so deeply that I could hardly speak. The audience was patient, and so was Ed. I shared the story of the abortions I had so many years ago. I had never shared this very personal information publicly before. As I continued to share, my emotions were so raw that two people from the audience came up to stand by me and served as support beams to help me finish telling my story to the audience. I eventually shared enough to reveal the painful scars that I carried for more than 35 years. There was a pastor in the audience that came up and prayed for me as I finished. When I composed myself, I raised my head from my chest to see the comforting faces in the audience. The audience gave me the strength to move forward with my head held high as I found my feet to walk to my seat. I grew stronger as each silent affirmation let me know that someone else felt my pain. Ed soon called for a break; I was relieved because I needed to regain my composure.

As I exited the room, so many people commended me on being brave enough to share my story. It was not until I went inside the ladies' bathroom that it all became clear. Standing at the sink while washing my hands, the woman next to me said, "I was raped by a doctor, and I never told anyone." Other women came to me and said they, too, had made similar choices to abort their babies. I knew they shared with me to give me comfort and to say, "You are not alone." As I prepared to leave at the end of the workshop, one of the trainers gave me a handwritten note which read, "The same thing happened to me." It was then that the lightbulb truly clicked on. There were hurting women in the room. Some far more wounded than I was. One lady shared how she had tried multiple times to commit suicide because of past molestations and rape. It suddenly hit me like a ton of bricks. As much as I wanted so badly to keep my story hidden, God wanted to use me to free so many women who were locked up in their self-made jails. These women needed to be released so that they could live the destiny and purpose God had designed for them to fulfill. Isn't it freeing when the secret is finally out? For more than thirty-five years I carried this unnecessary weight. One that was never mine to carry in the first place. It was God's job to do the weightlifting, but I took on the role of being 'god' and thought it was mine to carry. If I carried it, no one would ever know. I did not realize that all the while my burden was getting heavier and heavier day by day, month and year. There were times that the weight got so heavy, and I cried without explanation. By that I mean, I did not dare tell anyone the real truth of why I was really crying. God had to put an end to the weight of my secret. It was too much to carry around with me. He sent His Son to the cross for my sins and your sins. That's where I needed to leave my shame; at the cross, no place else. Even more impacting is the fact that God sent His Son to cover all the sins I had committed and the sins I would commit in the future. Yes, my dear readers, the cross is strong enough to move us from the place of brokenness to worthiness.

When I decided to leave my home in New Jersey and get a fresh start in Florida, I did a lot of soul-searching. Florida was a springboard for me. What I found after a while was a beautiful flower that started to bloom again. I learned very fast that fear and faith could not live in the same body. I had to break up with fear and embrace faith if I wanted to keep moving positively on my life's journey. Slowly but surely I started to see consistent steps of faith in many areas of my life. My trust grew in believing in myself, knowing I was not walking alone. I may be alone in the natural, but I am never alone in the spiritual. I saw evidence of my trust growing in God because my default to worry waned. Through much prayer and fasting and wet tissues, God began to deal with me; He dried my tears. I started to look at my life internally, more so at my core. I felt like the numbers were adding up on my age and there were callings on my life that God would hold me accountable for. I had to get my act together and get back up and focus on my purpose. In reality, I had to deal with my pain. My emotional pain, my financial and the physical pain of rapid heartburn or acid reflux as the doctor said. This was due to all the increased stress in my life. It was my first born son, John, who said, *"Mom, you got to let go of the blame you carry from your past. Think of it this way. If you had those babies, we might not have been here. Your life would have been different. You were young, and you made the choices without seeing where you would be today. Mom, don't look at life this way. Without us, your life would have been different."*

I suffered from people-pleasing syndrome during the battle to keep my experiences a secret like I was taught. Most times I offered half-truths to keep the lid on the poor choices in my past. I would give abbreviated testimonies in church or any gathering where women shared stories about their lives. By doing this, people were able to see where I was currently, but they had no idea of the pitfalls and detours of my life's journey. They made comments about how strong I was, but they did not know how much weight I was under or had been under because of my past. It was like a pressure cooker; one that could explode if not handled carefully. I was so conditioned to believing the lies of the enemy that people would shun me if they knew my truth. The false reality was so real to me that it caused me to stay quiet in my cell. My imagination ran randomly in my mind, and I stayed in my cell without realizing that the door was never locked. The door was only closed, and all I had to do was push through to my freedom. But I did not know it. That is what fear can do when you don't make the decision to break free. There is power in the first brave step toward freedom. That first step is made the moment you make a decision. Every step of faith after the decision will develop like a snowball. Years later, I realized that I should have walked forward toward God who had the keys to open invisible doors all along. I spent valuable time in my cell, not realizing that I could have left long ago.

The workshop opened my eyes and allowed me to understand how important sharing my story was; not only for myself but for the freedom of others as well. I finally saw how people who needed to take action and break their chains needed to see my resilience and hear how I created my freedom. How sweet it is to finally taste freedom from within. I realized now that all the tears I shed were watering seeds of resilience and freedom on the inside of me. I see the beauty of the pitfalls and detours now that my seed has grown into a beautiful flower.

God's footprints in the sand remind me that He alone carried me through the rough and bumpy patches of my life. He is still there waiting in the balance to take me through the rest of my journey. I see the beauty in my journey now because God is my partner and my pilot. I submit myself to His plans as He navigates what's ahead of me. My past mistakes did not break me, and I know that God is the only one who could have designed my present and my future this way. I am thankful to God for His forgiveness of my choice to abort my babies. I am thankful that He forgave me enough to give me two sons so that I could experience motherhood. Some people never got a second chance, but I did! I am also happy that during all of this turmoil, I did not experience deep depression even though my sadness was great. There were moments when I could not get untangled from the web of shame that was woven around me. In those moments, God provided healing through tears, and the special people He placed in my path who did not judge me.

I am thankful for the friends who prayed with me and allowed me to cry on their shoulders. Shame held me hostage, but thanksgiving was the light that broke through the thick dark clouds. The heart-wrenching pain made knots in the pit of my stomach which moved slowly to the rest of my body. I am thankful for the grace and mercy that covered me through the experiences and courage to help heal others. If we are not careful, the clutches of shame can get in the way of any destiny and assignment. But know for sure that God won't ask you to be resilient without giving you hope.

If Moses could not lead his people without first having an experience with God, why did I think I could? I had to stop and ask myself who I was and why I thought I would be exempt from trouble. Facing my gremlin gave me hope to embrace my purpose. I knew that I was to be used by God to assist others to find freedom from their self-made prisons. So many people have made life-altering choices that slammed the door shut on their future, or so they thought. Once I found my hammer and broke the chains, I became a willing vessel to be used by God. I serve as a guiding light of hope for women who are serving time for the innocent lives they took with the tool of fear. Because I am free, I can show others how God can wash and cleanse them to live and thrive again. My faith has shown me that I do not have to live a life sentenced to shame for past mistakes. God provides a redemptive resilience that can shorten any prison term. I use my own journey as a guidepost to show others that freedom is a by-product of resilience. There is victory if we just take the first brave step and come out of our self-made jails.

This new belief ignited a love for learning and a resilience that was essential for great accomplishments. A growth-oriented mindset creates motivation and productivity. It also enhances relationships and increases achievement. A growth-oriented mindset was what I needed all along. I thought I had it, but life got in the way. Or should I say I got in my own way with negative self-talk. My best friend, Joyce, encouraged me to try journaling.

I started to see it as a possibility when she told me that I didn't have to write a lot. She told me to start with a few lines and go from there. In my old mindset, I told myself I was not a writer. For many years I did not like writing and had a complex when it came to writing. I listened to the negative voices in my head that repeated what I had heard others say about my writing. I did not value my written words very much because I struggled with adding "s" where there should not be one. I talked myself out of the beauty of my written words. Thank goodness for my marital crisis. Putting pen to paper became a life-saver for me as I was going through all of my emotions that came from the pain, stress and frustrations of my changing life. I am a girl from the islands, and proper grammar can sometimes be a struggle. I began my writing journey with a gratitude journal where I made a commitment to write a few things I was grateful for each day.

Eventually, journaling became a systematic habit for me as I recognized how therapeutic it was. I shared candidly for healing while writing about my personal and professional life. Journaling gave me an outlet during the times I caught myself writing in between teardrops. My heartache was lessened as the tears smeared the blue ink of the cotton pages. The beach became one of my favorite places to release the pain. The calmness of the ocean and the roar of the waves provided motivation to express the thoughts that were doing tumbles in my mind. Most of the thoughts were about my dreams, family and life. Other times, I would sit in an almost fetal position on the comfy couch to deflate my aching heart. The beautifully colored journals welcomed my open heart. I poured my heart out where no one could see it but me, not knowing it would turn out to be one of my best healing processes. I allowed the pen to anchor on the pages and let truth flow like honey to the sweet place of release. Soon, I became braver and braver to talk about the things that were buried deep in my heart. I became my own therapist and had a journal for my aches, anger, hurts and frustration.

Joyce insisted that I get a pretty journal and write my gratitude daily. She told me, "Start with three things." I started with three, and before I knew it, I had a whole page of things I was grateful for. This practice eventually led to a new habit of writing 100 things I was grateful for each Thanksgiving Day. This was also another suggestion from Joyce. Everyone needs a Joyce in their lives. This is someone who comes along and makes a difference in your life. In 2013, when I developed this new tradition of writing a gratitude list on Thanksgiving, I wondered if I would be able to write 100 things, from the time I woke up until I was ready to sleep for the night. I would keep reflecting to write something I was grateful for. I could not duplicate lines on the list, so all of the gratefulness had to be original. As I watched the clock, I discovered how difficult it was to come up with the last 50 things without repeating myself. I decided to look at themes in my life to generate ideas for the last 50 things.

An example of themes would be what I was grateful for about home, work, specific people in my life, my car but most of all, me. Try it, and you will see how much you come up with about each of these entities in your life that you do not think about or ones you would tend to overlook. Like, for example, your feet. I am thankful for my feet daily because I can walk. There are people with feet, but they can't walk. There are people with no feet and want to walk. The Thanksgiving Day writing exercise is an intentional exercise. It pushes me to look at things through the correct lenses. There is a quote by Wayne Dyer which says, "If you change the way you look at things, the things you look at change." After reading this quote, I realized the need to look at things in my life correctly with intent. I still continue this heartfelt tradition today. My freedom continues with the positive therapeutic results I received from *reflective journaling*. This was recommended to the students of the John Maxwell certification program. In my three pages of reflective journaling, I had one

SHELIA MALCOLM

page for listing the things that went well. The next page was for what did not go so well. The third page was for the lessons I learned from what did not go well.

As I practiced these reflective exercises, I learned to look at things as they were, not worse than they were, not better than they were, just as they truly were. This exercise caused me to be honest with myself while being accountable and authentic. It also points me to the question of what I learned today. What is the lesson? When I get feedback now, I am not shocked at most of the comments anymore. This is because I have already given myself my own feedback. I strongly believe that self-reflection helps to encourage me in a very genuine way. It allows me to take responsibility for my mistakes and not to answer to the negative name calling from the other side of my head. When I recognize I made a mess of something, I ask myself the three reflective questions to come up with a positivity to learn from my mess. (1) *What went well? (2) What did not go well? (3) What can I learn from what did not go well?* The questions create a bridge for resilience. If you do not believe me, try it for 30 days. If you stick to the process, you will recognize how to intentionally become your truest authentic self. The more you reflect on yourself, the more you will see the change in you from the inside out. Everything that you will ever need God already put it within you. It can only be found when you become your own personal archaeologist. During this process, I refer to a quote by my mentor, John C. Maxwell, "Good leaders ask great questions." Don't be afraid to ask yourself questions and answer them with boldness and truth. This will help you become the change you are waiting for. Self-therapy through the journaling exercise is now part of my resilience.

In 2015 when one of my clients came to me, she was a director of a non-profit organization; she was struggling in her career and wanted to get a promotion ASAP. She filled out the intake sheet and we went to work. I was quickly able to identify

54

what was holding her back. The top results she wanted were: to build up her self-image, self-awareness and have inner peace. She had been divorced twice and she was an agnostic to name a few of her hurdles. I worked with her closely on bi-monthly calls for five months. In the sixth month she was on a webinar with a group of my students and she was so excited to announce that she got the promotion. She said she applied all the steps we established together. She said 'I can genuinely smile now. I'm at a peaceful place in my journey". Others have complimented her on her new normal. She started making time for herself and put herself first without feeling guilty. Another one of my clients is a teacher; she, too, was divorced with small children. She implemented journaling and music in her daily self-therapy practice. Her goals were to love herself again, enjoy the season of her alone time and get past the pain from her past relationship. She found a radio station that had a lot of positivity. She wrote her own quote that captured the result she wanted. She said it every day. It goes something like this. "May my heart be kind, my mind fierce and my spirit brave." Through our interactions together, before long, she was getting out of the house more. She was meeting with friends, participating in marathons. She was able to tap into the fierceness she always had on the inside. She just needed a coach to help her navigate her path and find this hidden treasure. You, too, can experience these same results and achieve your possibilities.

My confidence grew as I wrote and I realized I could write from my heart and my editor could help me become a great writer. My newly found growth-oriented mindset, combined with resilience convicted me to stop talking and take action in every area of life.

Once I quieted the noise about my writing, I went on to tackle speaking. I joined Toastmasters International to help combat my fear of speaking and to develop the tools I needed in my toolbox. I began to intentionally get out of my own way and truly free me from me. I started my writing by simply using journaling as another tool in my toolbox. I wrote speeches and presented them in Toastmasters. On that stage, helpful feedback came from the audience as well as from my mentor. I volunteered to speak at schools and a Women's Conference. I spoke at churches, and I taught leadership skills to people in and around my community. I spoke at different events around town for free. I even got brave enough to teach leadership webinars across several states virtually. These were all done with the aim of getting good while making a difference in people's lives, knowing I was getting out of my way and becoming the change I was waiting for. I carefully crafted my resilience bridge by being compassionate with myself and embracing my new mindset. At this stage of my life, my greatest motivator, Grandma Jane, was no longer here to remind me of all the affirmations she packed in my toolbox so many years ago as a child. I revisited the building blocks of my bridge and smiled at the necessary changes I made. I grabbed the very necessary tools to reignite my beliefs and positive thoughts of me. Resilience is not a one-time behavior; it is an ongoing process which I must participate in daily. So, I pull out tools from my unshakable foundation and apply them just as my Grandma Jane did when she faced adversities. The creative tools she used were not from a psychiatrist or a psychologist. They were tools she designed after taking a good look at the issues she faced; she would make a conscious decision to keep moving forward. She always believed in prayer and in a higher power. She snacked on scriptures nightly before heading for sleep. Even though the behaviors she practiced were impactful to her survival, I was now able to analyze that what I saw in my grandmother as her resilience came through self-therapy which she used throughout her life.

I lead my life through service while being fully committed

to my resilience. I have learned to be willing and unafraid to ask myself some tough questions that will unlock the doors to my potential. My continued freedom relies on my ability to answer each question with a clear heart, free from the chains of my past. This means I must always commit myself to letting go of anything that does not keep me free. Honestly, it isn't easy, but the freedom makes it all worth it.

SERVICE

"Live a life of substance through your service, your substance and your offering of your whole self."

—Oprah Winfrey

TAKING INVENTORY

THERE IS FREEDOM IN LETTING go, but there is also a cost, and it's not necessarily paid with money. Leaving my husband was not something I contemplated as I entered marriage. The possibility of divorce never came to my mind before my marriage because being a divorcee was not something I wanted to add to my personal resume. As I allow you an opportunity to get a glimpse of my life through my lenses, I want you to know departing my 24 year-long marriage was no celebration. It was very far from joyous! As I contemplate things I aborted in my life, I will say my marriage goes on the list. Toward the latter years of my marriage, my stomach bore evidence of the constant financial stress I went through. The pressure caused knots to build a permanent house in my stomach. The prolonged distress with little to no relief spiraled in acid reflux. Home remedies did not seem to work because I had not taken the first step yet. I took that step one morning as I navigated the turns on the curvy, narrow roads through the countryside in Hunterdon County, New Jersey. While in route to work on my 50-minute drive, I felt an intense pain in my chest and began to cry out to God. I remember asking God to be with me and not to let me die over this! I was frustrated about a lot of things, and they were starting to show up in my health.

When the challenges of life start to manifest in your body in a negative way, it's time to stop! Take inventory and make changes. The same way I had to change my mindset about my past abortions, I had to change my perspective about the 'D' word. I am not advocating divorce. But if the emotional, physical and financial costs are too great for you, your children and all involved, then you have to make a change. If you are married, only *you* will know if that path is for you or not. I chose that path which would bring relief emotionally and physically. The decision only came through intentional assessment to see things as they really were. This caused me to face the truth of where I was emotionally. I was torn, I was scared, and I had mixed emotions. The truth be told, I emotionally checked out of my marriage several years before I physically left my home. There was a progressive departure. I left my marital bedroom to the guest bedroom. Then I left from the guest bedroom out the door. The steps toward the door were gradual. They were the final agreements with my heart before my actions confirmed that I was done and it was indeed over!

I will never forget when I officially took the ultimate step out the door on August 25, 2012. In hindsight, it was two-fold for me to leave on the 16th death anniversary of my beloved grandmother, Jane. This was an eye-opener for me. I revisited that day in my mind many times as I went through the grieving process. I recognized that when I took steps to leave my marriage, I had to also take time to mourn the death of my marriage. When you mourn the loss of someone or something, you experience several emotions. Psychology Today outlines it best in providing these five stages of grief: 1—Anger; 2—Bargaining; 3—Depression; 4—Acceptance; 5—Denial. It confirmed the five stages someone would go through on the journey to their healing. These were also the same lessons I learned in the Divorce Care class I attended. I experienced every one of them, and some of them recycled and came around a second time.

The denial I experienced was one that shocked me. When

the temperature of my marriage shifted drastically in 2008, I sat up straight and put on my big girl pants. I did not think I could leave my marriage. In the early phases when the thoughts came into my head, I quieted them with questions like, "How are my children going to feel? How will my actions affect them emotionally?" Many times I wanted to deny how I was feeling and put my children before me. I wept and I wrote. Going through the exercises and sharing in the Divorce Care class helped me to see my denial clearly. Bargaining crept into my head many times, but somehow that thought did not last long. I did not linger at the bargaining table. Anger, hurt and disappointment quickly overruled, and so the cycle went for some time. I had many friends and family who prayed with me and for me. I know that was how I made it through my toughest time of managing these five emotions.

Writing remained as a pillar to my recovery, but I could not find my harmony during the height of my divorce. As much as I wanted to be grateful, it was difficult for me to consistently contribute to my gratitude list. I found myself so absorbed in worries and stresses that surrounded my finances. My mind was constantly weighted down with questions like: *will the mortgage be paid this month? Where are we going to find the tuition for both children in college?* The electricity was already cut off twice before, and there was still a huge balance. Borrowing money was not an option. The ability to repay was going to be a challenge for my lenders, the bank, family, and friends included. I was at a place where I was overwhelmed, and relief was desperately needed.

At one point, my sister visited from Scotland with her husband, and I had no electricity in my home. No one knew this and I was beyond being embarrassed. The foundations of pride were strong, but I knew I had to do something to redeem my self-respect. I swallowed my pride and went to Catholic Charities for help. I answered every question they asked about my finances.

I bore my soul as I provided supporting documents of all my past-due bills. The process brought me to my knees with the shame of not being able to take care of my home and my children financially. I was so overcome by my stressors that it became trying and the exact cause for the divorce.

Resilience kicked in when I decided to own what I had done without making excuses to give direction to my mourning the end of my 24 years as a married woman. This was my first step toward healing. There were days I wept sorrowfully at the state of my finances and emotions. I was starting all over again from scratch in a different state away from most of my family and friends. Even more heart-wrenching, I was a long distance away from my beloved sons. There were days and nights I cried myself to sleep. I was angry with myself for causing pain to my children. I was saddened by the state of my finances. There were days I woke up and wanted to go back to sleep immediately, hoping it was a bad dream. Even when I barely made it through, I rose to the occasion and served myself by accepting responsibility for my portion of the blame. The emotional wrestle was daunting as I identified causes for the breakdown of my marriage. The moments I spent with my grandmother kept reminding me that I could get up if I could look up and I started to take small baby steps toward healthier thinking and actions. I read my Bible several times per day; it was the antibiotic that aided in healing my infection. I listened to the audio version of Psalms to provide the comfort I so desperately needed. As I was going through the emotional episodes, I could now understand some of the emotions David echoed in his songs and prayers to God. God helped David, and I was depending on Him to help me too. I reminded myself that I wanted to get well as I prayed out loud and silently. I prayed even louder when I thought God did not hear me the first 32 times I asked Him to take my pain away.

When I felt like God did not hear me, I took some time to

examine my life. I took serious inventory of the different areas of my life as well but really focused on my spirituality because I was struggling to pray at the time. I considered myself a prayer warrior, and I ran to God with all my challenges as I constantly interceded for others. I am unafraid to express my appreciation to God for His goodness in my life. During my recovery season, I had difficulty getting my words out with conviction. I struggled to stay focused, and I fell asleep many times mid-sentence. My spiritual life was affected because I was not at peace. There was a battle going on in my head and in my heart. My destiny relied on my ability to sort out myself to reach others. With this realization, I became relentless in my wholeness pursuit.

The inventory continued as I dissected the financial pages of my life, and I did not like what I saw. According to the tax filing, our joint annual income was more than $200k in 2007; I was baffled because I was barely making ends meet. I pulled out all the stops to the relational areas of my life. I could not focus on intimacy. I chose to figure out how to get out of the financial hole we were now in, neck deep. I found it difficult to separate my financial life from my intimate life. I could feel the steam puckering in my throat whenever the phone rang, whether it was the landline or my cell phone. I was at my limit, and the steam could have blown off my lid at any time. I hated being at the mercy of my creditors. My financial situation was way past adding a Band-Aid. It needed surgery to stop the financial bleeding. As I slowly hovered over the magnifying glass in my marriage, I saw where I held on to the thought that my finances would get better because I had a direct toll free line to God. I believed that if I continued to pray and believe, my finances would eventually somehow magically become better. The part I missed from the verse was that prayer without works is dead. We needed to have an action plan for our family. Talking about it and wishfully thinking about it was not going to bring to fruition the better financial life I so desperately wanted. Prayer does not mysteriously fix a problem. I had work to do to bring my ideas to reality. I had a part to play in the realization of the kind of life I wanted to live. I have to do the work. The willingness to take a look at my finances offered me permission to use the avenue of bankruptcy to reset and start again. There was much struggle to swallow my pride and call the bankruptcy attorney to review my finances and outline some slow steps to my financial recovery. This action too, caused me to shift my perspective to the long-awaited relief I so seriously needed.

I mastered the skill of praying to God to forgive me of the choices I made and as soon as I ended the prayer, I would take my requests back from God and continue to worry some more. The behavior of constant worrying continued to multiply and spread into almost all areas of my life. I soon called myself a worry-wart. That title stayed with me for many years. Until one day during the onset of the unraveling of my marriage, I caught myself worrying about so many things that I literally got sick. One day while at home with my children, I started to feel severe pain in my neck. The pain eventually moved down my back. The pain was so excruciating that I lay across my bed and kept rolling from one end to the other, searching for relief. When relief could not be found, my husband at the time took me to the doctor. The doctor examined me and asked me a series of questions. She eventually told me that she could not prescribe me any medication for the pain. Instead, she strongly suggested that whatever I was worried about; I was to find a way to let it go. I left the doctor's office, feeling no better off than I did when I was rolling on the bed. I went to an acupuncturist for several months to try and use natural remedies. I took no medication reliever for my acid reflux, but after several visits, the acupuncturist said, "*I don't want you to waste your money. I can do only but so much for you. You must find a way to get rid of the stress in your life or lessen it somehow. Coming here to get this procedure will not help you. You have to deal with what is causing you the immense stress."* I took her advice, and I did not go back. I remained on pharmaceutical medications for approximately 5 years until 2013. I was desperate for a turnaround in my health and tried juicing and praying more. This helped me tremendously because I was now away from some of the things that caused me stress.

Later that week, I purchased a set of *The Power of Praying* books by Stormie Omartian. The collection of four books included, *The Power of a Praying Wife, The Power of a Praying Parent, The Power of a Praying Woman* and *The Power of a Praying Husband.* This was where I changed my diet and started to feed on words of encouragement, and relief came from these pages daily. All through my readings, I was still praying for God to change my husband and my situation but never once did I pray and ask God to change me. Halfway through reading *The Power of a Praying Wife* a lightbulb went on in my heart which caused me to shift my perspective and I started to pray and ask God to change me. As I continued to ask God to change me, I saw evidence that I was worrying less. My worrying was not all gone, but I was becoming more aware when I was being the 'god' in my life. This was where I wanted to fix the things that I had prayed to God and asked God to do. I wanted to take them back and fix them myself. Some of the things God allowed me to work on with Him as He provided me guidance to develop a healthier relationship with me. There were other situations I had to let go of so that God would work through them and show me the way. Through reading these books as well as many other books, I started to handle life's challenges more positively. It was during many of these tests and trials that I discovered a new love for reading. I read then as I do now for self-help and improvements. I no longer read any books that were not designed to improve my life and teach me ways to help me so I could help others.

Once I reached a place of peace in one area, I did a deeper

dive and found so many unfinished dreams and desires lying around. Then again, I put my health assessment under the microscope. There I found dissatisfaction running all over. I had acid reflux, restless night and the scary chest pain one morning on the way to work. The chest pain was the one that stopped me in my tracks, and the neon lights went on brightly in my head. I shared my views and thoughts about my overall observations with my spouse, but change never came. I prayed for positive change. What came out of my prayer time was, 'You cannot change people. You can only change you!' And there my intentional journey began, again. I stopped asking God to change my spouse, and I focused on the change in me. Dealing with the abortion of my marriage became easier once I understood my personal responsibility to serve and be served. With the bulb of awareness finally lit, I realized I could serve best on areas where I had experience with results of overcoming.

Once I acknowledged the service component, I became very intentional about becoming the change I wanted to see. I sought the freedom to embrace my truth without the baggage of shame. I craved environments where my words would not be placed under a microscope in search of points for misinterpretation. One of the things that frustrated me prior to exiting my marriage was the constant filter and pressures to watch my every word. I did not want my spouse to feel like I was sending out 'smoke signals' to people about what was going on with our marriage.

Anyone who knows me will agree that I like to testify in gatherings. It can be at church or just a group of folks hanging out together. I will not hesitate to testify because I love to brag on God. Just seeing how God keeps me through all my tests and life challenges pushes me to gratitude. Spiritual balance is important to me and should be important to you too. Your whole self (spiritual, relational, financial and wellness) should be in alignment to experience the success you yearn for in this life. When we engage in the evaluation process, we identify areas in need of service as well as the strengths we can serve from.

During my inventory, I realized that I was disconnected from my true self. I am not saying that if you experience disconnection in your relationship, then you get a lawyer and head for the divorce court. But I do encourage self-evaluation within any relationship to ensure its health. For me, the divorce process was very painful, and while I knew it was the best for me, I did not only think about me. My role as a mother is to serve my children with love in a healthy environment, and I thought about my children more than anything before and after I left. Several things kept coming up. As I divorced hopelessness and began my path to a whole life, I realized the importance of a solid support system. Healthy support systems provide the outlets for routine service maintenance. Rebuilding my life required me to lean on my friends, the God-given ones.

Joyce is twenty-two years my senior, but sometimes I forget because she is so current with the latest trends and technology; I can hardly believe she is in her seventies. I am not sure exactly how we became best friends but we have so much in common, it's scary. She is an encourager and a Prayer Warrior. I think this laid the groundwork for our friendship. I can remember times when I was going through tough decisions or had to face my truth, Joyce was there for me and with me. Most times not physically in my space but virtually connected. God is Center of it all to us. Everyone needs a Joyce in their lives! She serves in love and motivates me to always reach for the best within me. As our friendship grew, at times we paused to reminisce and asked each other, how we met and couldn't seem to remember, but what I did remember was that we met at church in New Jersey. We eventually started working together on the administrative team as the church clerks. Joyce is brutally honest and refreshingly authentic. She is logical in her thinking and unashamed of being vulnerable. She may not be these things to all people, but she is all that to me. I believe God put her in my life as a bridge to help me navigate the challenging waters I would have to cross.

I can remember many times when I was overwhelmed by life's challenges; I called Joyce on the phone. And she always listened attentively. Then she would say, "So, what did you learn from that?" Or "How does it make you feel?" Each time she asked these questions, she did not necessarily need me to answer right then and there. Sometimes it was more of a rhetorical question to help me ponder inside and get in touch with my truest feeling at my core. There were other times when she just listened to me cry. Sometimes I was like a weeping willow, but she gave me grace. Grace to be me, grace to eat a slice of humble pie and grace to speak without judgment. Joyce always had a parking space for me marked, "Judgment free zone." With that space for honesty and truth, I had the opportunity to acknowledge my hurts, my pains, and my truth all at the same place. God knew I needed her and He sent her in my direction. We have been friends for more than fifteen years and counting. There were times when I could not pray for myself or the situation I was facing because I was gazing at the glass half empty and seeing all the negatives that were not even present. In those times, she stood in the gap for me and prayed me through. This is why I say that Joyce is the kind of friend everyone wants to have in their lives. She is my confidante and one of my biggest cheerleaders. She is in my 'front row.' Joyce lives the testimony of the Titus 2:4 woman, the one where the older women must train the younger women to love their husbands and their children.

Just like my grandmother, Joyce is resilient and strong. She also used our time together for teachable moments as she armed me with lessons from her life. How she navigated the troubled waters in her past. She used her life experiences as teaching tools for me to hold on to as my anchor. When I first began contemplating my divorce and even after I left my marriage, she always served up a healthy dose of self-evaluation. She had been married twice in the past, but both marriages ended in divorce. One would think that when it became my turn to face the challenges in my marriage, she would advise me to leave. She did not. As I would share the broken-hearted version of my pain, she would often ask, "So what was your part in it?" "What have you learned?" One day, she did surprise me by making a statement instead of asking me questions. I can't remember what my drama was at the time I shared with her, but she said: "You will know when you have had enough!" She never once told me to leave my marriage. It's not her style. She loves marriage. Even though a third opportunity has not arrived yet, she still believes that if it's God's will, she will welcome it. Joyce's gift is sending cheer and building hope in the wavering heart. Joyce is intentional in strengthening our friendship. She practices this with things like baking my favorite coconut cake or baking my new favorite Chinese noodles cookies wrapped with butterscotch and sending them in the mail. She would send me surprise packages of goodies if she knew of someone passing near where I lived. Even though we are so far from each other, it feels like she is still within miles of me. So many times I would go to my mailbox to be surprised by cards in the mail. Joyce finds the most situation-appropriate cards out there. The messages are so personal and so profound that I sometimes wonder if she has a direct connection with the card manufacturers to print the right card that speaks into my soul. I love cards, but so many times I can't seem to find the right ones with the right words. I want those cards that sound like how my heart is feeling toward the situation or occasion for which I am purchasing the card. Joyce just has a knack for words. God always provides a ram in the bush. Joyce is my 'ram' and I thank God every day for her.

I know you might be wondering why I shared so much about

this in the chapter on service. Well, I would admit that I had no idea how to serve in a friendship capacity until I met Joyce. I wanted to help others, but I didn't always know how to help myself. Maintenance of my freedom from self was connected to me understanding how to serve. I am grateful that God knew I needed to feel it to give it to others.

As my friend and author of *The Unexamined Life*, George Casey, Jr. said, "I believe it is my divine mission to challenge myself as well as others to better your best while never leaving one's life unexamined." I truly believed that taking time to do the inventory into my life thus far caused me to pen these pages. My inventory led me to actions, and the actions were rooted in service. I have learned to forgive myself and become vulnerable about my journey so you may find your wings whenever you decide to fly. I flew higher than ever when I forgave myself for everything that didn't help me serve others or myself. Forgiving oneself is huge because there is no way you can help others if you are not willing to pardon your own mistakes.

I made a deal with God to not only live for Him but to serve and praise Him in all I did. The deal was to praise instead of complain, worry or be caught up in a whirlwind of things I could not control. I told God that instead of falling apart in my tests, I would serve Him through my gifts. Almost immediately after consciously making that commitment, I noticed a change in my speech as tests and trials knocked on my door. Instead of going in the place of panic, fear or possibly a temporary state of depression, I chose to ask God what the lesson in that situation was for me. I learned to get busy working before the fear offered negative chatter of my worth and value.

To move forward, I anchored on HOPE, my favorite word. There was a twist to my anchor. There were days I felt hope-*less* when looking at what was before me. I had less of a lot of things. Like, my broken relationship, my dismantled finances.

My children were far away, and so were my friends, my church family and anyone that was close to me. I looked hard and deep and could not see hope anywhere nearby. I had to reach back again to the foundation my grandma helped me build. I had to divorce the *less* off my hope and start to find ways to be full again. As I started to see evidence of my joy returning, I added '*ful*' to my hope and became hopeful. I got my genuine smile back.

Looking back now, I ponder the truth of being pronounced pregnant at 13. I still experience quiver and nervous butterflies doing summersaults in my belly even though I am free from the chain. Throughout the process of writing these words as part of my self-therapy, I wondered what I could have said to my thirteen year-old self when I realized I had missed my menstrual cycle. I spent time lingering over all the interrogating questions from my grandmother as she tried to put all the pieces together to then establish that I was pregnant. During my questioning, I was nervous and very scared. I was outright naïve to get myself in this precarious place. I relied exclusively on the assessment and words of my grandmother and instantly believed in her pronouncement. I never went to a doctor nor did I take a pregnancy test to confirm that I was indeed pregnant. I knew she had my best interest at heart and held on to my belief in her as I reluctantly drank the horrible tasting herbs she boiled repeatedly for a week.

As I ponder on the power behind service, I can see how knowledge shines a light on the area of struggle to help create the right perspective. Had I stayed bound to my past mistakes, it would not have been a good place to serve from. While writing this book, I decided to do some research on the internet around the subject of girls experiencing irregular periods. Oh, how I wished I had internet access in 1981. Not only did I not have a computer or the internet, but I also did not think to go to the library and research this compelling question. According to *Kids Health (.org/Pamf.org)*, "A girl's body may not follow an exact schedule. It's common, especially in the first 2 years after a girl starts getting her period, to skip periods or to have irregular periods." I also asked my friend who was a pediatrician, and she confirmed that it was not uncommon for young teen girls to have irregular periods. I was amazed by the information I found in my search.

Learning this information caused me to wonder even more, what if I was not really pregnant. I needed to know this in 1981. It may be late for me now, but it is not too late for the girls I will encounter in the future. I continued my quest for more understanding, so I read several articles on the American Journal of Obstetrics and Gynecology website as suggested by my pediatrician friend.

I often wondered what I could have told my thirteen year-old self, to be fair to me, knowing that hindsight is 20/20 vision; I had to be honest but truthful to me. This is where the forgiveness piece fits into my life. Since my knowledge about relationships, the development of my body was so limited then, I had to gently offer grace to me. I know better now, therefore, I do better. I have accepted the fact that what happened to me was part of the process to make me stronger than where I was at thirteen. I decided to let it go and draw from it even though I chose the wrong path to becoming sexually active as a young teenager. God is using me today for His service to help others who may face similar circumstances. Knowing what I know now pivoted me to ask myself if there were other areas of my life where I held on to the wrong perspective for too long. God giving me the opportunity to become a mom, not once but twice was a joyous experience for me. So many times over the years, I heard stories about women who had abortions and lost the chance to give birth when they thought they were now ready to embrace motherhood. That thought lingered in the back of my mind. I had to talk to myself several times to let go of tomorrow's worries and fully serve today from my dreams and gifts. Having this knowledge revealed to me, caused my perspective to shift again in a direction to serve women and girls who can benefit from my experience to create a brighter future for themselves. I believe that whatever gifts you are blessed with, they are not for you to keep hidden. You were given those gifts to be a ray of hope for others. Healing is tied to service, and we can only serve effectively after inventory has been taken.

Identity Formation

What do I say to myself?
How do I see myself?
Fearfully + Wonderfully
Made,
uniquely crafted.

I lean on God
for perfection
always. I am
patient w/myself
Grace/kindness
laugh at my
mishaps/mistakes
Forgive myself
Reflect on my
sins/don't sulk
in my emotions
"Keep moving."

THE POWER OF PERSPECTIVE

SERVING ON ANY LEVEL IS a big deal! From helping the less fortunate to leading an organization, you will need compassion and resilience as you lead. When you step out to help those in need you are putting others first and addressing their needs. You are saying by your action that you want to make a difference in their lives in a positive way. At the root of the service, you are stating by your actions that you want to make things better for the people you are serving. I have found that most people give from their greatest area of emotional need or lack. Of course, it may not always be true, but one thing remains, everyone should serve with purpose. Wouldn't it be nice if the server served from an authentic place?

For many years, I often wondered what my purpose was on earth. It took me a while to fully understand or even truly appreciate my purpose. But one thing is certain, from the beginning I knew it was not about me! As a child growing up in the countryside with my grandmother, I witnessed love in action. She was constantly doing whatever she could to help others. Her spirit of love and compassion is engrained into the very fabric of my being. So much so that I often find myself doing the same things she did when she was alive. I'm constantly giving myself, whether it's sharing my time, my food, my space, my knowledge and even my funds. History is repeating itself. What I saw my grandmother do, I had emulated without realizing how impactful her actions were on me.

I realized that walking in my purpose means being intentionally kind even when it was inconvenient. There is a deep sense of satisfaction I feel when I help those in need. At one point during my major life reboot, I started to feel alone. I knew that I had to find a positive outlet for my feelings to be redirected, so I began to share with seniors at a facility. Ministering to the residents in the nursing home blesses me just as much as it blesses them. Seeing them smile when I offer words of encouragement and sing songs of joy brightens their day and reminds me of times I spent singing with my Grandma Jane. Many of these residents do not have families who come to visit them. To be honest, there are times when I have looked at them and realized that it is only a matter of time before my mother may be in a similar situation. I gave from an authentic place at the thought of my mom depending on others to help her, and it also provided me with a glimpse of what could be ahead of even me. Will I be lonely? Will my family visit me? As these unnerving questions run through my mind, I realize that I have no control over what the future holds. I redirect my energy to service by living in the present and making a positive difference for others.

I am constantly shifting my perspective while walking in my purpose. I feel a great sense of satisfaction that I am able to provide a glimpse of hope, joy, or even peace for these residents; even if it's just for a moment. These same feelings resonate within me whenever I'm preparing and serving meals to the homeless. From time to time, I remember that when I give to the least of these, I am giving unto my Father in heaven. I strongly believe we can help shape our world positively through effective change. Acting on this belief for several years, I committed myself to partnering with the senior leaders of Jacksonville Job Corps. I committed to volunteering and assisted the students with building a changed mindset to help better their future. On a weekly basis, I would impart to them strategies on how to develop positive thoughts of themselves as leaders. They focused on mastering the core values in the skills they were developing to use in their future workplaces. I taught them how to extract the lessons from their life experiences and to live confidently through them for empowerment. The art of this teaching was to help each student see the value in what they might have viewed as a negative story. Eventually, most of them understood their power to stand on the truth of who they could become through life's experiences.

We are all designed to make a difference in the world; one compassionate act at a time. One compassionate act of service can go a long way. A simple smile, a kind word, or even a good deed can be life-changing. An act of kindness can change someone with thoughts of nothing to live for. Service to others creates an atmosphere of gratefulness for all who enter. Intentional kindness can shift a mindset from a perspective of hopelessness to a positive posture of hopefulness.

As I reflect on my purpose, I am reminded of an experience that will forever be etched in my mind. It was a beautiful sunny afternoon in 2010, I was excited to leave work early that day, but it was for a sad reason. I was going to Brooklyn, New York, to a viewing for the mother of my sister's best friend. This was supposed to be surprise support for Tonya. Tonya is my youngest sister's best friend. My sister lived in Scotland and could not attend the funeral of her best friend's mom. I thought I'd go and represent her. I did not tell Tonya I was coming because I had not seen her for more than 20 years, and I wanted to surprise her in her time of mourning. Unfortunately, I never got to Brooklyn, all because someone's perspective of looking at the glass half empty took charge of the moment.

The unthinkable happened just as I got off the bus and walked toward the waiting room at the Hamilton train station. I was minding my own business and not really focusing on my surrounding when suddenly a woman to the right of me began to scream. Her face turned bright red, like a tomato and she began to hyperventilate. I rushed to her aid as she almost fainted and helped her to find a seat in the waiting room. Her companion got her a bottle of cold water to aid in calming her down, and I felt comfortable enough to walk away from the situation. I wanted to know the cause of the commotion that began just as I turned my back to help the woman. Feelings of confusion filled me as I passed onlookers who were crying and screaming in despair.

To my amazement, I realized how God shielded me from witnessing a horrible moment which would forever be etched in all the onlookers' memories. While I assisted the ill woman, an Acela Amtrak train was coming down the track at more than 100 miles per hour. As it whizzed by, it crushed the body of a woman who had lost all hope and jumped in front of the oncoming train. I will never forget the sound of the grinding screech of wheels against the iron tracks. The train operator tried, to no avail, to break the momentum of the speeding train to stop it before hitting the woman. The horrible sounds of the people on the platform screaming in disbelief drenched the atmosphere. The scene was too gruesome for me to describe to you. It was similar to road-kill splattered across the highway except it was a human. Her blood, bones and identifiable body parts laid splattered on the track. She was now a memory.

But because I was intentional in walking in my purpose of service, I was sheltered from the traumatic sight the onlookers experienced.

HOPE REVEALED

HOPE FILLS MY SOUL WHEN I think of Grandma Jane. She lived the word HOPE in her actions and through the gifts she shared. My grandmother taught me so much wisdom, and I really did not realize, as a child, the powerful testaments she planted in my life. Only now as an adult as I chat with family do I see the depth of what she imparted to me and all those she ministered to. I know your environment can make you or break you, and I am a living example that my environment did not break me, but it made me stronger. In all of the challenges I face each day of my life, I know that God gave me an earthly teacher who used every moment of our time together as a teachable moment. There is a famous saying that "*The fruit does not fall too far from the tree.*" If I did not believe it I'm living it. I often catch myself reflecting similar things that Grandma Jane would have done. My home has an open door policy just like hers. I often refer to it as 'Penn Station.' Anyone can come by for something to eat, a place to rest temporarily or a place to come to and get away from it all.

The things she did for the people in her community are the same types of things I do for those I interact with. It's a trait that ran through my grandmother's veins, and she passed it on to me. Not by transfusion or spoken instructions but by way of her actions. As if that was not enough, I have seen where my younger son displays these acts of service now. My children have a soft spot toward helping those in need. I clearly see how the legacy of my grandmother trickled down from me into my children. The residue of service is sprinkled all over them. In 2014, my older son volunteered with his alma mater, Penn State University, to raise money for the Four Diamond Fund to help children who were battling cancer. That year the event raised more than $13 million. I watched my son go through the grueling 46-hour commitment of no sleep, all for "the kids." Even though he was tired and wanted to quit, he kept his mind focused on the goal. He came to the point of tears many times during the 46-hour dance-a-thon, but he stood strong. His commitment fueled his mission to serve the children who were depending on him.

The strong support system gave him visible power and supernatural strength. I watched him being lifted onto the backs of his Sigma Nu fraternity brothers for relief from standing. They inserted unexplainable encouragement for him to keep going. I even stood with him 25 of the 46 hours. As his mother, it was amazing to witness the changes in his perspective during the experience. His mind shifted from his pain and lack of sleep to the ultimate goal of pushing through to the end. Each time he felt the nudge to sit down and call it quits, his little two-year-old buddy that was battling cancer gave him the second and third winds of hope he needed to keep going until the end.

If you were to ask my younger son what hope looked like, he'd say it's chasing an elderly man who was eating from a garbage can at the Metro Park train station to give him his last $10. He knows that hope can make a difference even in something as small as a meal. When I looked back on the event which unfolded that day in the train station, I credited his behavior to God. Hope requires serving actions, and he rose to the occasion as God spoke to his heart for a response in kindness. When he returned to the car after catching up with the elderly man, tears poured done his face. He asked why is it that, in a place like America, people have to eat from a garbage can? I had no answer; however, I joined his heartfelt hurt to see such sadness on the elderly man's face. I was so moved by his compassionate heart that I cried along with him. My mind replayed the elderly man's face as he kept staring in the direction of my son. He stood almost in unbelief with a lingering look maybe to say thank you to an obedient young man that allowed God to use him. In a split second of the elderly man turning around, he disappeared into the darkness of the dusk.

It's a good thing my younger son is strong-willed; sometimes it works in his favor. On another occasion, he had an opportunity to help a young man the same age as he. This young man was struggling to break the debilitating chain of drug use. Even though my son's circle of friends shared the opinion that becoming this guy's friend was not the thing to do because his choice to use drug would eventually affect my son who was not a drug user. His friends shared many non-supportive comments to deter him from helping his schoolmate. My son saw through all the hurt and pain of this young man to defy his friends' feelings, and he reached out and showed him hope through service. He encouraged him to get involved in sports, write music and find other non-destructive ways to deal with the void he was trying to fill. My son served him despite the discouragement of others.

So, what does **HOPE** look like? It looks like anything that changes lives to make a positive difference. **HOPE** is someone believing in you even when you don't believe in yourself. Hope is courage to stand in your own light away from joining your circle. It's the strength to walk alone to help someone break free from destructive behavior. **HOPE** is holding steadfast to that feeling in your gut that says, "You are being asked by God to make a difference right where you are even if you don't have the support of the crowd." **_HOPE_** is having someone to cry to without feeling like you have to stop because you're using all their cell phone minutes. My journey has given me hope to not only live but to grow and thrive. As I hold on to hope, I remind myself to keep taking my medicine for total health. With this in mind, I began music therapy as a vitamin to keep my perspective positive.

Can you imagine a great movie without phenomenal music to set each of the scenes? Music can set any scene from revealing that something scary is lurking in the next clip, to the hype up-tempo music to create the excitement of what's to come. Just like in movies, music often declared the atmosphere of what was going on in my life. I had to find more tools to help me stay true to myself and keep my promise about minimizing my worry. Music became that tool, and I now saturate my soul with it.

Even though I don't play any musical instruments, a variety of music can be found on my Pandora® radio stations and iTunes playlist. I have a different type of music for every mood I experience. When I am cleaning my home, you will hear a wide array of music if you pass by. The carefully selected mixtures serve as motivation as I sweep the floors or fold my laundry. I allow my spirit to soar with the winds of each genre change from reggae to fast-paced Latin rhythms. They all keep me company and help me to get through my chores with efficiency. Since it is my daily vitamin, the K-Love radio station plays 24 hours a day, 7 days per week in my home. I submerge my mind with music at all times. When I write, classical instrumental pieces of symphony excerpts play lightly in the background. I am encouraged with every dance of the artist's fingers across the ivory keys. This is a safe and healthy outlet to calm my frazzled nerves.

For me, music is renewable energy just when I need it most. Music has been my homeopathic medicine for many years. When I am down, music picks me up. When I am in the place of worship, I am open to hearing the voice of God through my worship experience. At times I find myself singing to the top of my lungs in praise and worship to God in my most sacred place, the bathroom. That is so funny to me! The most interesting thing is I get my greatest revelations and life-changing thoughts in the bathroom. The conservative scholars may point out that connecting with God in the bathroom may not be the most revered place. But for me, that's where God meets me most of the time because it's a distraction-free zone.

I dance and sing on top of the music oozing from my iPhone and get carried away when William McDowell starts to share prophetic words for healing. I was brought to tears the first time I heard William McDowell's intro for his song, "Give us your heart." I felt like he was speaking directly to me at the moment. He said, "Your time of public revealing is coming faster than you have time to prepare for it." As I continued to listen, he simplified it for me. He said, "The reason you are needed soon is because there is a Goliath in the field challenging the armies of God and you are the only one who knows how to kill it." The Goliaths he mentioned were poverty, homelessness, hunger, loneliness, and abortion. I concurred with him on all the Goliaths he mentioned. But when he said the word abortion, I instantly felt he was speaking directly to me. It was something I could absolutely relate because I had experienced it. This caused me to stand at attention because I knew that Goliath! I continued to listen for more revelations and William continued to prophesy. This song intro was speaking life into me and calling me to say yes. My yes was to the artfully framed marching orders. I had to serve with the understanding that there were many women in the pews who were crying on the inside but smiling outside. They felt chained to their past just as I did and unable to get beyond the mistakes they had made. There were also men who wished they could go back and change the decision their girlfriends or their wives made in the past. But they were not able to, and they suffer silently for being part of the decision to not let their children live.

Abortion is one of those untouchable subjects that most churches avoid. It's a quiet storm that so many people face every day and try hard to put it behind them. Most times, they cannot because of the feelings of shame and worry what 'people' may think of them if they get to know them. The intro for the song by William McDowell continued, and he shifted the perspective by proclaiming *"there is a new generation emerging that is going to slay Goliath."* This is what powerful perspective does. It challenges change and service to the atmosphere. This revelation made me change the way I thought about myself. I began to understand what he meant in saying, *"You have to believe you can change the world. You are not just dropping a pebble in the ocean, and nobody notices. If we adopt the negative worldviews that say things are only going to get worse until Jesus returns, we are missing it. Jesus said we have Authority! He said we have dominion. If it gets worse, it is because we allowed it to. God wants to raise up a generation that is on an assignment and believe that we can change the world with the authority of God,"* Something rose up in me as William shared these words. They caused me to shift my perspective and take my place in God's army. He has equipped me to serve his people, supported by the authority of God.

Songs with profound messages speak to my soul. They call me to take responsibility for where I am, and they remind me of where I need to be. As I continue to take my daily doses of musical medicine, I can see where I have grown. I have improved in places where I may not have paid attention to, but the lyrics of these songs call them to attention. I can go on and on about the many different songs that have spoken to my subconscious mind, causing me to keep my promise to stay on the path of my journey. This commitment to service and self-care sealed healing in the depths of my heart.

God will use whatever He has to amend those broken, insecure places in your life. If you are on the search for healing and wholeness just as I once was, I encourage you to listen to the song titled *It's not over When God Is in It* by Israel & New Breed. Let me share a few sound bites of this song with you until you get a chance to listen to the entire song. "*Seasons are changing, everything is different now. It's not ending it's only the beginning, It's not finished. When God is in it, there is no limit,*" as I heard these lines I knew this too was part of my marching orders. The marching order was to recognize that my life was not over because I decided to have an abortion. I had to forgive myself, let it go and be an ambassador for God. I gave myself permission to help other women who might be experiencing the same battle. I listened to these songs; it's as if they were written for me and they were literally singing directly to me. As I worshipped and cried out to God for help to move forward with joy and peace, the lyrics bathed me. The songs were symbolic and assisted in washing away my shame and condemnation. They gave me the power to embrace a new perspective sealed by the fact that God could truly use me.

If you talked to my sons today and asked them to list a few things that their mother did which they did not like, among their top five things would be, "My mom is very defensive." Defense was my mechanism to protect and cope. After the death of my Grandma Jane, in 1996, I would eventually conclude that no one really protected me as she did. No one really fought for me. I felt that truth deeply, I had to fight for myself. Survival was almost always at the top of my list of things to do. As I practiced my survival skills, I found myself apologizing repeatedly. It was not until years later, after intentionally doing a deep dive in and through my life, that I discovered why. In my subconscious, my grandmother was my She-ro. I found no one else willing to protect me and love me unconditionally as she did. Not my mother, not my father not even the man I eventually married. Of course, this was my perspective before God got my attention and shifted my heart and mind. God only needs a second of attention to draw in our hearts.

From music to the simple things we often overlook in life. I'm reminded of this when I think of eyelashes. How can something as simple as eyelashes draw you in? My firstborn shifted me into the rhythm of motherhood with deep respect and realization of the power of God. It was neither his nose nor his face that pulled me in, but it was the beauty of how his eyelashes curled. They were thick, and they lay so beautifully on the lids of his eyes. I've often heard that the eyes are windows to the soul. I was mesmerized by its beauty. How could someone so beautiful come from me? How is it possible, God? Slowly, over time, I wept silently for robbing my other babies of the life they could have had. When my firstborn moved inside my belly for the first time, I felt intrigued by fascinating tingles yet still hidden from view. When his beauty was revealed at birth, all I could have said was that 'it was totally amazing." God's handy work prevailed. Who am I to make a choice to rob little voiceless ones from being a part of the plan of God? Only after tearfully dealing with the pain of abortion, did I realize why God allowed me to go through this process. It was for the purpose of being used by Him with grace to be a benefit to others. Those who are still locked up in the "what do I do now?" prison or the "what have I done?" jail.

My God said, "*Shelia, you are up to bat, now hit the ball out of the park. Hit a home run for Me! What you've been through is for Me.*" It's always been about Him and not me. If this applies to you, I urge you to get your healing and get ready for your next assignment. Please know they won't always be easy or even pleasant at times, but you are built for this moment. God created you to stand strong at this moment. Remember His promise to you in **Joshua 1:9:** *"Be strong and courageous."* He also promised to never leave you or forsake you. Just as He was in the fire with the three Hebrew boys, He is with you today and for all your days to come.

You are the vessel He wants to use to bring comfort and peace to those assigned to you. You, my darlin' daughter or son, must be willing to serve as God's willing vessel. Stand at attention and accept the brave honor of the calling placed on your life; you are here to serve Him, just as Jesus served the Father in heaven to bear the sins of this world. There will be moments on the service road where your cross may seem heavy, but you have been given the victory to overcome whatever cross God allows you to bear. Jesus is with you just like God was with Jesus on the cross. Your journey is specially designed just for you, and you have power from within. If or when you get scared, remember that God will be right there with you. It is important to soak in the reality that you must know you are not carrying your cross alone. Jesus had help in carrying His cross, and He has already carried yours to Calvary.

The final shift in my perspective came when God confirmed that I was doing what He called me to do. He reminded me that it was my job to be His hands and feet and go joyfully to share with the women and girls who needed to know that their jail cells were open. When I serve, I reboot the power to tell others that they too can be free. My experience taught me that only God could set you free from the bondage of sin. Jesus knew because He carried it for the world. It got so bad that He asked God the Father to let Him out of it. God loves us and does not like to see us in anguish; He was silent when Jesus suffered because He knew the freedom of the world depended on the sacrificial service. There are so many in need of healing but run away from God because it seems like He is silent during their struggles. Silence requires a perspective change from feeling ignored to pushing through. I'm right here with you in the valley. You will get the strength to climb and just know it's going to be all right. Take the chain off your mind, change your perspective and live!

LEADERSHIP

"A leader leads by example,
whether he intends to or not."

—Author Unknown

REDEMPTION

WHEN I LIVED IN NEW Jersey about six years ago, I shared with my sons, Johnny and Matthew that I was going to speak to youth in the schools and the community to try to help them. They were excited for me, but they wanted me to *keep it real.* They wanted me to know that they appreciated experiencing my gift of encouragement throughout their lives. And they provided valuable feedback in saying that they warned me, that only genuine transparency would work. My bold and beautiful son, John, asked me what I was going to say. Then he reiterated his point in saying, "*You know you have to be authentic because kids can see right through you if you aren't honest with them.*"

Hearing these words of wisdom from my then 18-year-old son, I started to ponder whether I could help the kids in his school and in the community without really telling them my story. I took a pause—a really long pause. It was so long that I discarded the idea of asking their principal for permission to speak to the students. I truly believed that I could share my insights about the other parts of my life story without telling them my deepest struggle and shame. If I only picked and chose the good parts of my story while leaving out the horrible parts, my journey would be incomplete. The thought of leaving out parts of my story left that empty nauseating feeling in my gut which was what would make my story worth telling.

My childhood memories of my GM were awesome. The memories of her loving leadership provide redemption in the times when I feel saddened by her absence. During the Christmas and Easter seasons, she would bake cakes and Toto (sweet coconut bread) in the community brick oven, and she would purchase the largest bottle of Red Label Wine. She would make sure the single elderly folks in the community had some cake and a shot of wine if they wanted. My grandmother had a BIG heart. She was an investor; one who believed in putting things aside for a "rainy day" (i.e., emergency). At times there were shortages of many necessary products on the Island, such as kerosene oil to keep the lamps lit at night and for the stoves to cook nourishing foods. We had shortages of salt and flour just to name a few. Even though these times came around quite often, my GM never got caught without. She believed in buying extra and putting aside in case of emergency. She not only had extra for herself, but she would also share with folks in the community. She was a leader in her giving and always gave what she could to those asking her to share her portion. I remember her words with each gift, "*I don't have much but here, pinch it.*" The folks in the community respected and admired her for her preparedness and her ability to lead through service in the community. She loved to cook, and she would always cook the main dish in her 3 legged cast iron pot on a wood fire. As a kid, I always wondered why she cooked so much food; we couldn't eat it all in one day. When I asked her, she would always say, "You never know who is going to stop by; you'll feel ashamed if someone stops by and you do not have enough to share." This was definitely a teachable moment for me, which is why I still do it today. I always cook with the thought in the back of my mind that someone may stop by and I should have enough to share. My GM had such great qualities because she believed in brightening the corner right where she was. She was a true leader and made a difference in somebody's life every day; it was her spiritual gift.

I'm truly amazed at who I am now and to see this shy, bashful, naïve and short little girl from Jamaica now with an enthusiastic, passionate voice offering words of encouragement to all. The leader I am today operates with forward faith. Forward faith operates in the positive opportunities of now instead of the past or pain. I've truly transformed into a beautiful butterfly not without pain which has carved my purpose. My forward faith allows me to sprinkle a ray of hope into the lives of my children, friends, family, colleagues and those who come into my personal space. Many times, I find myself writing a few texts or penning a few words of encouragement to people whom God places on my heart. My encouragement allows me to be a leader in every situation. I realized I had this beautiful gift that God hid way down deep within me that was wrapped in shame. I naturally wear a smile as part of my wardrobe. I believe it's the topping of the artistry of a beautifully dressed woman or a handsomely dressed man. When you add a smile, it changes everything.

As I watched my life transform over the years, I learned how to identify my spiritual gifts and the natural God-given talents which come easily. I recognized that when I got excited about something, it was *like fire shut up in my bones*. At times if I'm not careful, my passion can come off a bit preachy. I leave the physical fighting to my God and King to fight my battles as He promised in Exodus 14:14. I've seen where I have grown from calling a friend to share the impact of a negative comment or a negative experience to calling on King Jesus first. I have learned to run to my God because He made lots of promises and I've finally grown up enough in them to know now that every one of those promises is true if I only believe. God does not lie. He has promised to take care of things for us all if we just stand still and submit to His leadership. This does not mean literally standing without doing your part of the work for the process to work. Standing still means—continuing on with God even in the face of doubt, detours and plain old tiredness from having to get up so many times from falling down.

When the enemy brings up the fact that I had abortions, the loving Father counters them with calm, soothing voice saying: *I have used men in the Bible who have committed similar crimes, talking the lives of the innocent and I've used them mightily because of their repentant hearts. You are no different, Shelia! Allow me, the Potter, to refine you and use you for my glory. The poor choices you made were all part of God's process for my Purpose.* He reminds me that each scar shines brightly through the forgiveness of Jesus and His redemption for me.

On April 4th, 2016, the birth of my first grandchild, Grayson Bennett, created a shift in my Divine Detours. Withheld tears in my eyes for several months gushed out, not out of pain or anger but out of what I called a breakthrough. This is something I have felt deep in my gut from the night my son, Mattheu, told me his girlfriend was pregnant. He's telling me after only finding out himself that his girlfriend was pregnant and he did not really know. After going through moments of saying out loud OMG to my son telling me I'm going to be a grandmother. The rest of the week, I wrestled with the thoughts and questions like, "Couldn't he at least wait to finish college?" I did not really spend a lot of time thinking about Grayson's mother's well-being. Several days in after the initial shock wore off, I slowly began to think of Grayson's mom. I wondered how she was doing. I wondered how her family received the news or how they reacted to her. For the first time, I put myself in 'her shoes.' For a moment, I began to have flashbacks about being pregnant in my teens. It's too late to have an abortion now even if she wanted to. In between my own ranting in my head, reality struck me. Well, at least she has broken the cycle of abortions in my children's family. I felt like her finding out late that she was pregnant was a blessing in disguise for me. Why for me? I don't really know, but that's how I felt. I never asked my son about their choice if they were going to keep the baby or not. I knew in my heart it was a given. This was God's way of saying, "Shelia, the chain has been broken over your family." After a little while passed, I reached out to Brekke, Grayson's mom, and said hello. We briefly exchanged texts. I eventually asked her for her mom's cell phone number. I felt that as woman to woman and mother to mother, we could have a dialogue about our children. What can I say to this dear lady about my son and her daughter's choice? I chose to just say hello through text at first. We picked a time for us to talk, but life got in the way. After several days I sent her a text message to ask if it was a good time for me to call her; she agreed. I called, and her first words were "I love your son!" What a way to break my anxiousness of what to say to the mother of a daughter with a bright future ahead of her which will now be detoured for a little while to nurture and care for a baby.

As I had more time to talk to my son, and to Grayson's other grandmother, I started to develop this sense of peace in the midst of what could have been a very chaotic family situation. There were lots of emotions on both sides as to why our children allowed passion to overcome them. Brekke's mom shared that her daughter was still on track to graduate from college in 2016 with three degrees. "She is usually very well organized and has her head on straight; I don't know what happened to her." I echoed, questioning myself. The months to come after the birth of Grayson, reconfirmed my sentiments of God's great sense of making something good come out of things that may not have started out so good. Seeing pictures of Grayson and getting updates from his mom and hearing the joy in my son's voice truly convinced me that Grayson was a gift from God and he would be a delight to all or even if it's only for me. He was <u>a sign that the abortion chain</u> <u>had been broken over my seed.</u>

Grayson and I already have some wonderful things in common. <u>He is my first grandchild.</u> I was the first grandchild for my paternal grandmother. Grayson has two <u>grandmothers</u> with very similar names. His maternal grandmother's name is <u>Sheila</u>, and <u>my name</u> <u>is Shelia.</u> At a glance, you may be tempted to say he has two grandmothers with the same name. Just so he's not confused, I've told him to call me "G-Ma." He has truly broken the chain for me.

My first encounter with Grayson, the weekend of July 8th, 2016, was far more than I could have imagined. As the white Crossover pulled up, there was a sense of hopeful excitement that filled my heart. What was only two months and a few days felt like a year. The beauty in his sleepy eyes slowly unfurled with a yawn that said, "I'm awake, just a little bit." I could not wait to take him out of his car seat. As I was about to take him out, Brekke gave the disclaimer, 'He might be a little fussy because he's not feeling well.' I proceeded anyway because I was overjoyed and excited to see my little munchkin, Grayson. To hold him in my arms, I looked past his eyelashes and saw his contagious smile. He pulled me in almost immediately. The beauty of his one dimple on his right cheek melted my heart. The dimple on his face reminded me of the one on the face of my one-dimpled navy blue-eyed grandmother. For what it's worth, Grayson and I connected immediately. He did not cry nor did he fuss. It was almost like our hearts synchronized to love on each other. For the next hour, his mother and father had no opportunity to hold him. This behavior was definitely unlike the childhood experience of Grayson's father and uncle. They were criers. They did not go to people unless it was their mother or father. Grayson was a breath of fresh air. Grayson's uncle and I took turns looking in his eyes, smiling in amazement as to how sweet and cooperative he was. He had not fussed or got annoyed with us for going gugu—gaga over him. It was as if he recognized that we were kindred spirits. *We were one with him.*

REFLECTIONS & GROWTH

AFTER COMING TO AMERICA IN July 1981, I had a few dreams. Distinctively I wanted to learn to drive after graduating college and bring my GM to the USA so she could experience what an airplane ride was like. As God would have it, I was able to do just that for my GM in November 1988. Enjoying an airplane ride in her mid-sixties, my GM felt very special. Finally, she was able to not just look up in the sky at airplanes flying overhead, but she could now share an experience of coming to the United States of America. I remember as a child, my GM often shared stories about my parents traveling on an airplane to where they lived. After my GM's first ride on the airplane, I came to realize that she really enjoyed flying. Consequently, she took a few more airplane rides, one for my wedding and one for her medical treatment when she was diagnosed with Alzheimer's in 1996.

In 1991 when I got married, my grandmother baked my wedding cake. When I tasted the sample cake, it took me back to my childhood days when she would bake in the community oven, and she would give me batter mix left in the mixing bowl. I also would be the first to get a taste of the mix and also of the baked cake. It was amazing to have her make my wedding cake.

It showed she still had it going on. That was the last time I really enjoyed her baking. It was not too many years later while she was home in Jamaica, I started receiving very disturbing messages of her possible declining health. In April 1996, her nephew, Danny, whom she also raised, brought her to me in New Jersey, so we could have her health evaluated. It was then we heard the very sad and disturbing diagnosis.

When we were told of her Alzheimer's, it broke her heart and ripped mine to pieces. As I saw the tears welling up in her eyes, she asked, "What did I do to deserve this disease?" All I could do was cry with her because I too saw the effects of the fast-moving disease. The charming, strong, one-dimpled lady was now experiencing short-term memory lapse. The woman I looked up to was now facing the challenge of her life. My GM had never been sick in all my years living with her. The only other time she was down and out was when her right foot got caught in the spokes of the motorcycle on her way home from a funeral. This incident happened when the motorcycle she was on as a passenger fell into a huge pothole and her foot slipped off the pedal and got cut. During this experience, my GM walked on "all fours," and she continued most of her regular weekly schedule except for traveling to the market and to the river.

What I learned from my GM during those times was that she never let anything hold her back. What she could not do, she was not afraid to ask for help from her family and friends. I saw determination and strength as she swung up and down the stairs of our home. She was focused on getting to the kitchen to still prepare meals for her family. She was the epitome of the strength of Samson in my eyes. So many people would possibly have given up or made excuses. At times when I would say to her in my childish words: "GM why are you doing so much and you are sick?" Her response would always be, "It's my leg that's sick, not my mouth or my hands. Whatsoever your hand findeth to do, do it the best you can without complaining." Those were her words of comfort and edification. You could not help catching her contagious positivity. This is why the shock of Alzheimer's penetrated her body and started the vicious invasions of robbing her of her agility and spunk she had with her creative mind. This was a shock to her being. My heart leaped in my chest to see my GM change right before my eyes into someone who now had to depend on me and others around to remind her where she was or where she was going again and again.

She did not live very long after being diagnosed with this terribly debilitating disease. In June 1996, she returned to Jamaica after spending approximately three months with my family and me in New Jersey. When she returned home to Jamaica, she could not live alone, so she became a resident of a nursing home in Westmoreland, Jamaica. This was hard for my GM because she loved her home and her independence. I visited her in July of 1996 and spent 3 weeks with her. Upon my departure, she said, "Shelia don't forget me!" As I write this quote, my eyes are all welled up with tears. I never thought this strong, one-dimpled, navy, blue-eyed woman would be in a state where she could not take care of herself. This was a strange place for her because she had lost her independence. I know her request was not to make me feel guilty but to remind me to still consider her a part of my daily thoughts. How could I have forgotten such an awesome mentor and GM? This was the last time I saw her alive, but we kept in touch by phone for the next few weeks before she departed this life on August 25, 1996.

I have drawn strength from the foundation my grandmother laid for me at an early age. Many days when I sit and reminisce about the opportunities I was exposed to growing up, I am grateful for the lasting impressions I carry with me daily. Sometimes I look at today's children and shake my head in dismay with how they are being raised or even how they behave. Children today tend to have fewer restrictions and have learned fewer life skills that can be of benefit to them as they grow into adulthood. As I see these behaviors, I shake my head and say, "If they had a parent like my GM, they would not do that." I am honored to carry on the pillars she instilled for my unshakable foundation. She will forever be remembered for the love she gave through service and her demonstration of leadership through compassion and resilience.

Grayson has given me the privilege to explore my new world of freedom as a grandmother. From the moment we met, he recognized that we were family and innocently led me into a new phase of growth, free from myself and the chains of my past.

If today your heart is aching, if you are about to throw in the towel and are wondering how to get back up again, I offer you these **tools** to add to your toolbox. **Find a coach**; someone that can help you identify where you are and devise a plan to get you on your path to recovery. That place where you will find a healthier you—physically, emotionally, financially or spiritually. A coach keeps you accountable and encourages you with every step you make in the direction of progress. **Don't give up!** Start talking to yourself. Speak positive words out loud every day so you can hear them. **Thank God for what you have now.** Thank Him in advance for all the things you want to see, feel and experience in your life. Be specific, call them by name. For example, God . . . I want to love myself more. You can say . . . I am strong. I am joyful. I am unstoppable. Say the words for what you want in your life. As you speak these positive words daily, you must take action at the same time. If you want better financial results, take a budgeting class. Go to your local library and take some of the free courses they offer on a wide range of subjects. That's what I did. Many people are not aware of these free services. If you want to start a business, they have courses for that too. **Find inspirational quotes specific to the situation you are trying to**

solve in your life. Write them out on index cards. Read them out loud daily. Commit them to memory. These will help to motivate you. **Write 3 things in your Journal daily that you are grateful for.** Don't over think it. Keep it simple at first if you find it difficult. For example, I am grateful for life. I'm grateful for my feet because I can walk. Then build on your list as you reflect over your life each day. My grandmother gave me a great foundation so when I got into those painful places I was able to draw from them. I know, you may not have had a grandmother like me or anyone for that matter who affirmed you but you can do it yourself. Why? God already created you with it on the inside of you. Now look within and find it! I believe in you. If you don't use these suggested tools in your life, regret is the next hurdle you may face and that is so much more painful. Remember, it's ok to fall but . . . it's never ok to stay there.

EPILOGUE: LOOK WITHIN

IN NOVEMBER OF 2013, I was sleeping on the couch, enjoying my newly found intentional habit of taking a siesta on Saturdays after lunch. Before I drifted off to sleep, I wrote several names of what I should call my business; none of them really impacted my heart. I soon drifted off to sleep. I could hear myself muttering, "Lord give me a name!" When I woke up, the name came to me! The name the Lord gave me was *Look Within*. When I analyzed the name, Look Within, it was perfect. The name covered all aspect of my journey. I have been a wife, and I am a daughter and a mother. In each of these roles, I have experienced tests and trials. The one thing that has undergirded me as a constant thread of action was to look within.

Since you stayed the course to read my story, start to visualize you telling your own story. Not necessarily the same way I did nor to the people I told my story. What I need you to do is, see your story for what it is. You did not have the experiences you went through to stay quiet and keep them to yourself. Your experiences are for others. They are waiting for you to share and set them free! Is it you, or a member of your family? Is it your spouse or your child? Remember there is strength in being vulnerable. Decide today to free yourself from anything that is raising its ugly head to silence you. There is someone waiting to be released from their ball and chain of experiences life served them. Mine was the wrong mindset, abortion and divorce. What's yours?

Let the truth be ever present in your walk. Allow hope to be your anchor as it was for me. Brave the storms of your silence and use boldness to grant relief to those who are waiting for you. There is no gain without pain. The gain I speak of is not necessarily monetary. It's the gain to now be able to look yourself in the face and see past your freckled skin or the mole on your face. You see the good and the bad, and you love them both because had it not been for the bad, the good could never be. Your **mess** is your **message**, and your **test** can be your **testimony**. Why not borrow some of my faith and hope until yours improves?

To look within is to have a visual like standing on the arched bridge over the Wekiva Springs and looking over the wooden rails into the water. There, looking back at you is your reflection. It is not distorted. It is like a mirror. In the crystal clear water below, you will see as I saw, opportunities, like leaving a legacy for Grayson and my future grandchildren. I want all my offspring to know I was here. I want them to talk about me at their dinner tables, or while they share with others about the rich heritage their grandmother left them as my grandmother did for me. I want my future family to know I left footprints for them to follow. They can look at their lives and say to themselves that they too can rise from every mistake they have made or will make in the future. They can borrow encouragement from Maya Angelo's poem, *Still I Rise*. They will know that their grandmother was intentional in leaving them a legacy to anchor and rise upon.

So, what are you waiting for? Embrace "the you" from

within and take the time to look on the inside. You will have to do the work; I can't do that for you. But I can hold your hand with hope as your witness. What are the chains in your life that you need to break? Find the hammer you need to break the chains. It's in you! Look Within!

ABOUT THE AUTHOR

Shelia Malcolm is an International Bestselling Author and an award-winning Toastmaster. She is a certified Transformational Coach and Inspirational Speaker of The John C. Maxwell Team. She facilitates workshops to empower women to build their get-back-up-again muscle. Family is her first priority. Giving back and making a difference in the lives of others, brings out her passion for life. She is the owner and President of Look Within Life Coaching LLC. She resides in Jacksonville, Florida.